Watching DALLAS

WATCHING
DALLAS

Soap opera and the
melodramatic imagination

Ien Ang

Translated by
Della Couling

METHUEN · London and New York

First published as *Het Geval Dallas*
by Uitgeverij SUA Amsterdam
© 1982 Uitgeverij SUA Amsterdam
English translation (with revisions)
first published in 1985 by
Methuen & Co. Ltd
11 New Fetter Lane,
London EC4P 4EE

Published in the USA by
Methuen & Co.
in association with Methuen, Inc.
29 West 35th Street,
New York NY 10001

© 1985 Methuen & Co. Ltd

Photoset by
Rowland Phototypesetting Ltd,
Bury St Edmunds, Suffolk
Printed in Great Britain by
Richard Clay (The Chaucer Press) Ltd,
Bungay, Suffolk

*British Library Cataloguing in
Publication Data*

Ang, Ien.
Watching Dallas: soap opera and the
melodramatic imagination.
1. Dallas (Television program)
I. Title   II. Het geval Dallas.
English
791.45'72   PN1992.77.D3

ISBN 0 416 41630 6
    0 416 41640 6 Pbk

*Library of Congress Cataloging in
Publication Data*

Ang, Ien.
Watching Dallas.
Translation of: Het geval Dallas.
Bibliography: p.
Includes index.
1. Dallas (Television program)
I. Title.
PN1992.77.D3A5313   1985
791.45'72   85-15481

ISBN 0 416 41630 6
    0 416 41640 3 (pbk.)

Contents

Preface

When I wrote the original Dutch version of this book in 1982 I had several things in mind. I wanted first of all to intervene in the heated debate on *Dallas* in the Dutch media, which, to my mind, was characterized by a certain measure of ignorance, whether deliberate or not, as to the cultural specificity of this widely popular but highly controversial television serial from the United States. I wanted to encourage serious reflection on the phenomenon itself and, in order to do this, I deemed it useful to introduce the interested Dutch reader to theoretical perspectives on television and television serials, perspectives which stem mainly from Anglo-Saxon media and cultural studies. Dutch intellectual communities were largely unacquainted with these theories. The book, therefore, acquired a somewhat 'pedagogic' character.

Apart from presenting a framework within which *Dallas* could be taken seriously, however, I also wished to contribute to further problematization and understanding of the social, cultural and political role of serials like *Dallas*. Thus, I also deal with issues which come to the fore as soon as one adopts a position acknowledging that *Dallas* does matter, especially bearing in mind its popularity: issues concerning pleasure and its vicissitudes, its relations with ideology and cultural politics. Parts of the original text were more or less extensively re-written in order to overcome the difficulties arising from its originally being written within a Dutch national context. *Dallas*, however, matters internationally and it is my belief that the Dutch experience is not altogether a unique one.

Of those who have made this translation possible, I should especially like to thank Paul Willemen and Jessica Pickard. There were many others who supported me in one way or another in pursuing the project: Mieke Aerts, Tjitske Akkerman, Jane Armstrong, William Boddy, Christine Gledhill, Dick Hebdige, Johan Meijer, Antoine Verbij and, last but not least, the readers of the women's magazine *Viva*, who so kindly wrote to me about the (dis)pleasure that *Dallas* had afforded them. I am grateful to them all.

I.A.
Amsterdam, May 1985

Introduction

The moment of DALLAS

If we are to believe the plethora of studies, commentaries and warnings from journalists, critics and even politicians, the beginning of the 1980s was marked for the world's television viewing public by a new, spectacular phenomenon: *Dallas*. This unique status is due first and foremost to the extraordinary but undeniable popularity achieved by this American dramatic serial about a rich Texan oil family. That popularity has been wellnigh worldwide: in over ninety countries, ranging from Turkey to Australia, from Hong Kong to Great Britain, *Dallas* has become a national craze, with the proverbial empty streets and a dramatic drop in water consumption when an episode of the serial is going out. In the Netherlands, for example, over half the population watched *Dallas* every week in the spring of 1982, when its popularity reached its peak. No other fictional programme, foreign or domestic, has ever achieved such high viewing figures.

This almost inconceivable popularity has caused *Dallas* to

develop into a modern myth. It became the symbol of a new television age. Euphoric articles were written, especially in the serial's country of origin, on the success of the *Dallas* phenomenon. *Time*, for example, asserted with satisfaction in a cover story that 'the program's high gloss handsomeness brings a touch of class to the ruck of commercial series TV'.[1] But this American pride is countered in the rest of the world by quite different preoccupations. Of course, the Western European popular press was fascinated by the success story of *Dallas* and eagerly contributed to the myth-making. In more serious circles, however, its very success and popularity were fastened on for renewed expressions of concern over the steadily growing influence of American consumer capitalism on popular culture. *Dallas* was regarded as yet more evidence of the threat posed by American-style commercial culture against 'authentic' national cultures and identities. In February 1983, for instance, Jack Lang, the French Minister for Culture, during a conference in Paris to which he had invited a selection of prominent intellectuals and artists ranging from Ettore Scola to Susan Sontag, had even proclaimed *Dallas* as the 'symbol of American cultural imperialism'.

Of course, the problem raised here is real enough. On the eve of a period in which the structure and organization of the world of mass communications are about to undergo drastic changes, through the advance of the so-called 'new technologies' (cable, satellite), national governments and media institutions find themselves compelled to reflect on the social, political and cultural consequences involved and on the policy measures to be taken at this level. If nothing is done, the assumption is, the dominance of the American culture industries will just grow and grow. In this context the *Dallas* phenomenon functions as an alarming bogey. As Michèle Mattelart has put it, 'It is not for nothing that *Dallas* casts its ubiquitous shadow wherever the future of culture is discussed: it has become the perfect hate symbol, the cultural poverty [. . .] against which one struggles.'[2]

But the mere idea of a threatened 'cultural identity' contains elements which do more to conceal than to clarify the nature of the phenomenon and the problems described. Mattelart *et al.* have pointed out how, in the name of its defence, policy measures have been adopted which will not contribute to real alternatives.[3] It can, for example, lead to a misguided form of protectionism, based on a static, exclusively territorial definition of 'cultural identity', such as the setting of a quota system on imported films. For example, British television is allowed to fill a maximum of 14 per cent of its programming time with foreign programmes. But it can also lead to an unoriginal and unimaginative copying of American success formulae, so that viewers are served up a Dutch or French version of *Dallas*, which will inevitably be of poorer quality than the American original, for the very simple reason that the Americans have far greater financial and organizational means of production available. An average episode of *Dallas* costs at least $700,000, which the television industry of a small country like the Netherlands could not possibly afford.

Moreover, a stubborn fixation on the threat of 'American cultural imperialism' can lead one to lose sight of the fact that since the 1950s the mass consumption of American popular culture has been integrated to a greater or lesser degree into the national 'cultural identity' itself, especially in Western Europe. As a result, the popularity of a programme such as *Dallas* becomes a totally incomprehensible and elusive issue, a whim of the 'silent majority'. It becomes hard to understand, in other words, why such a large section of the television audience *en masse* watches *Dallas*. Often this position does not seem to get beyond the somewhat rueful realization that non-American peoples have a 'disturbing susceptibility to American media products'.[4] But this 'disturbance' probably looms only in the ivory towers of the policy-makers and other guardians of the 'national culture'. In the millions of living rooms where the TV set is switched on to *Dallas*, the issue is rather one of pleasure.

For we must accept one thing: *Dallas* is popular because a lot of people somehow *enjoy* watching it.

On the other hand we should not make the opposite mistake and let ourselves be blinded by the fabulous popularity of *Dallas*. The enormous fuss made of it can easily lead to a mystification of the phenomenon, to considering it as something unique. The temptation is great to reach for essentialist explanations, which are both too general and too specific. For example, the exceptional attraction of the villainous J. R. Ewing, one of the main characters in *Dallas*, is often cited as an explanation. Or, as the American television critic Horace Newcomb has done, an essential narrative foundation is sought that is assumed to express the Zeitgeist. According to Newcomb, *Dallas* succeeds in an inspired way in transplanting the old values of the Western into the new world of the American West, the world of express highways and stunning skyscrapers. He asserts: 'Probably without knowing it, the show's creators pump nourishment into the audience's veins. Their timing is perfect. As a nation we are actually growing older and developing the caution that comes with age. It is a time of decline, of recession and restriction, a time of real trouble. The grand old cities of the East and the Midwest are burdened with financial failure and bitter winters. Small wonder that the Sunbelt flourishes and *Dallas* leads the ratings.'[5]

This is all well and good, but the 'Americo-centricity' of such a speculative explanation totally loses its force when the worldwide success of the series is at issue. It is in any case somewhat risky to trace the appeal of *Dallas* to one hidden message or meaning, for it is not plausible that Moroccan, Italian or English viewers are all just as open to such a 'message' as Americans are – if indeed we could even lump all Americans together. The oil industry, for example, does not have everywhere the charged mythical significance that it has in American cultural history. Furthermore, popularity is never the unique accomplishment of one isolated cultural product. It is also dependent on and connects with the context in which it is consumed. In this connection we must not forget that people have become so used to American television programmes – their production values, their style and pace, their language – that merely the expectations they arouse and their familiarity give any new American product a certain advantage. None the less, this does not get over the fact that *Dallas*, just like Michael Jackson or E.T., has exercised a particular fascination exceeding the cultural significance of the average popular cultural attraction. On the contrary, *Dallas* appears in some way or other to have appealed in an exceptional manner to the popular imagination, although – just like any fashion – this is now on the wane. Stuart Hall has described how the popularity of *Dallas* in Britain peaked and declined: 'At a certain moment the programme achieved a kind of popularity other than merely in terms of numbers of viewers. It had repercussions on the whole culture, the involvement of the viewers became of a different order. At a certain moment you could no longer avoid talking about the popularity of *Dallas* when people started using categories from it to help interpret their experiences. This is a secondary type of popularity which it has now completely lost. The same number of people still watch it, but it is no longer active in the collective cultural consciousness.'[6] *Dallas* is nowadays, then, simply a popular television programme. Where viewing figures are concerned it has even been beaten in several countries by one of its own imitations, *Dynasty*.

In short, popularity is an extremely complex phenomenon. No simple answer is possible on the question of why *Dallas* is (was) so popular, just as it is not possible to explain fully how it is that Michael Jackson or E.T. have exercised such mass attraction. Very divergent factors, including historical ones, contribute to this, and it seems almost pointless to try to examine the success of *Dallas* without taking into account the wider social context of the postmodernist media culture. This book sets itself a more modest role. No attempt will be made to give the definitive answer to the burning question: why is *Dallas* so popular? Instead I want to concentrate my attention on a phenomenon, one aspect of popularity which is in itself complex enough: pleasure.

However, before turning to this topic, it is necessary to first describe what viewers are offered when they watch *Dallas*. As it is the way in which this programme is received and consumed which will be the focus of this study, I will not go into its production context here. I will confine myself to giving a short and simple summary of the *Dallas* story line; a more structural analysis of the programme will follow in the next chapters.

DALLAS: television fiction without an end

Dallas is a continuous fictional television serial which can, in principle, go on *ad infinitum*. The story centres around the very rich Ewing family who live in the luxurious Southfork Ranch, situated a few miles outside the city of Dallas (Texas).

At the beginning of the story, seven members of the family are living in the ranch: Jock and Ellie Ewing, the parents, their sons John Ross (known as 'J.R.') and Bobby, with their respective wives Sue Ellen and Pamela, and Lucy, daughter of their wayward son Gary.

The dramatic complications always revolve around the weal and woe of this family. J.R. plays a central role in this; he runs the family concern, Ewing Oil, in a villainous manner, treats his wife like dirt and only shows respect for his parents when it suits him. But it cannot be said that J.R. plays the main part: all the other characters in principle are just as important. Jock is the patriarch of the family who, around forty years ago, came to seek his fortune with his friend Digger Barnes in the oilfields of Texas. When success came he dropped Digger and set up Ewing Oil, which has since developed into a powerful concern. Furthermore, he also pinched Digger's girl friend, Ellie Southworth, daughter of the owner of Southfork Ranch. Ellie married Jock but has continued to have a soft spot for Digger. Meanwhile Digger has married another woman, Rebecca, and had a son and a daughter: Cliff and Pamela Barnes. Fate (or the plot) wills that the beauteous Pamela marries Bobby Ewing, Jock and Ellie's youngest son. Thus Pamela finds herself in a difficult predicament: on the one hand she belongs to the Barnes family and is loyal to her father and brother, on the other hand she is married to a scion of the Ewings, something her brother Cliff in particular cannot stomach because he is firmly resolved to avenge his father and destroy Ewing Oil. Cliff Barnes and J. R. Ewing are arch enemies. Cliff tries to fight J.R. through his work as lawyer and politician (something he hardly ever succeeds in doing because J.R. always manages to outwit him), but also by beginning an affair with J.R.'s wife Sue Ellen. The latter lives on a war footing with J.R. but also quickly gets fed up with Cliff. She is in a constant state of crisis: she goes to a psychiatrist, takes to the bottle from time to time and would like to leave J.R. but does not know how. Pamela has had more luck with Bobby, although the fact that she cannot have children (she has had a few miscarriages) casts a shadow over the happiness of their marriage. Fortunately her work for a fashion shop offers her some diversion. Meanwhile Lucy, who is around twenty years old, lives her own life. Now and then her father Gary comes back to Southfork Ranch with his wife Valene. He had previously left because he wanted to have nothing to do with the oil business of his father and J.R. (Here Bobby occupies a middle position: he likes the cowboy life on the ranch but is also fascinated by the modern business life in the city.) Gary is the favourite son of Miss Ellie, who is also suspicious of the oil business because it lays waste the virgin land around the ranch, and she sees the disintegration of the family with regret. The ranch is run by the cowboy Ray Krebbs who, surprise, surprise, later turns out to be an illegitimate son of Jock's.

As can be seen, mutual relations are extremely complicated. This is made even worse by the fact that from episode to episode secondary figures keep coming and going. For example, there is Kristin, Sue Ellen's sister, who starts an affair with J.R., but tries to shoot him when he deserts her; Alan Beam, a puppet of J.R., who is given the task of getting rid of Cliff Barnes, makes up to Lucy in the hope of getting rich through an advantageous marriage (which does not come off); Donna Culver, an honest businesswoman and politician who, after a short, unsuccessful affair with Cliff Barnes, marries Ray Krebbs; Dusty Farlow, a rich cowboy who falls in love with Sue Ellen, tries to get her out of J.R.'s grip but at the crucial moment has a flying accident and becomes an invalid; and Mitch Cooper, a poor medical student who gets hooked by Lucy.

This is only a brief summary, jotted down around half-way through the second *Dallas* season (at the time when I began this study). Since then relations and details have kept changing. Jock dies, not long after his former friend Digger. Sue Ellen divorces J.R. but not much later marries him again. Pamela and Bobby's marriage enters a crisis. Pamela finds her mother Rebecca again, who appears to be very well-to-do and is the head of Wentworth Industries, which are brought in by Cliff Barnes as a new weapon against J.R. And so on and so on.

But the basic structure of every *Dallas* episode always remains the same. In twenty to thirty short scenes the complications surrounding each of the characters are set out. In each episode a main story-line can be distinguished from a number of secondary stories. One main story, for example, is that Miss Ellie discovers a tumour in her breast. In various scenes we get her reactions to this: her fears, her visit to the doctor, the wait for the diagnosis, her doubts about how she is to tell Jock about it, and so on. Between these scenes there are others keeping us up with the lives of the other characters – for example, how Dusty and Sue Ellen are getting on, how J.R. pulls off his latest tricks, how Pamela indulges her 'mother instinct' by looking after Sue Ellen's baby, and so on. The number of locations for the action is limited: most scenes take place in recognizable locations such as the various rooms in Southfork Ranch and in the city of Dallas (the Ewing office, Cliff Barnes' flat, various restaurants, etc.). Nearly all the scenes consist of conversation; what we see the characters doing mostly is just talking to one another. In these discussions problems and mutual conflicts are expressed, generally of a psychological nature. Physical violence, and even milder forms of action, play a marginal part in *Dallas*. And this continues endlessly, in one episode after another. When one problem is still unsolved, another looms on the horizon.

Although this ever continuing story may sound ridiculous and terribly exaggerated to the disengaged reader, it is treated in an entirely serious manner within the programme. All themes and events are dramatized without any humorous distancing devices.

As far as visual style is concerned, *Dallas* offers no surprises: there are hardly any unusual camera movements, no experiments with lighting and so on; there are no diversions from the normal conventions of the production rules of prime time television programmes. In short, *Dallas* is in every respect an expertly made sample of mainstream Hollywood television.

Watching DALLAS: pleasure and ideology

Why do people watch *Dallas*? Clearly because they find it enjoyable. Nobody is forced to watch television; at most, people can be led to it by effective advertising. What then are the determining factors of this enjoyment, this pleasure?

Sociologists often start with the premise that media-use is determined by people's needs and the gratifications they expect. However, the attention given to the socio-psychological constitution of (individual) viewers implies a functionalist conception of pleasure in which its essence is regarded as the experience of satisfaction whenever a certain pre-existent need is fulfilled. What is completely ignored in this conception are the *mechanisms* by which pleasure is aroused. What are the characteristics of *Dallas* that organize the viewer's pleasure? This question indicates that pleasure must be conceived of as not so much the automatic result of some 'satisfaction of needs', but rather as the effect of a certain productivity of a cultural artefact. Evidently, *Dallas* offers entertainment, but what is it about *Dallas* that makes it a favourite item of entertainment, and what precisely does its entertainment value consist of? How, in short, does *Dallas* present itself as pleasurable?

In order to answer such questions we should not inquire what are the social, economic and psychological characteristics of the public, but should rather ask ourselves what happens in the process of watching *Dallas*. It is in the actual confrontation between viewer and programme that pleasure is primarily generated.

In order to obtain information on the way in which people experience watching *Dallas*, I placed a small advertisement in a Dutch women's magazine called *Viva*, which read as follows:

> I like watching the TV serial *Dallas*, but often get odd reactions to it. Would anyone like to write and tell me why you like watching it too, or dislike it? I should like to assimilate these reactions in my university thesis. Please write to . . .

I had forty-two replies to this advertisement. Letters, all addressed personally to me, varying in length from a few lines to around ten pages. All the letters except three were written by individuals. One letter was written by two boys and two girls, two letters by two girls. Only one letter was anonymous, all the others were provided with the sender's name and in most cases the address too. From these names it emerges that only three letters were from boys or men. The rest were written by girls or women.

These letters form the empirical material on the basis of which I shall be trying in the following chapters to say something about what it can mean to watch *Dallas*. Of course, these letters cannot be regarded as representative of the way in which *Dallas* is received in general. Nor can we assume that they are speaking for the way in which a specific social category (women, for example) handles *Dallas*. Interest in this study, however, is based not so much on the quantitative demographic distribution of the different ways the programme is received. Rather the central question is *how* these letter-writers experience *Dallas*, what it means when they say they experience pleasure or even displeasure, how they relate to the way in which *Dallas* is presented to the public.

It would, however, be wrong to regard the letters as a direct and unproblematic reflection of the reasons why the writers love or hate *Dallas*. What people say or write about their experiences, preferences, habits, etc., cannot be taken entirely at face value, for in the routine of daily life they do not demand rational consciousness; they go unnoticed, as it were. They are commonsensical, self-evident; they require no further explanations. This means that we cannot let the letters speak for themselves, but that they should be read 'symptomatically': we must search for what is behind the explicitly written, for the presuppositions and accepted attitudes concealed within them. In other words, the letters must be regarded as texts, as discourses people produce when they want to express or have to account for their own preference for, or aversion to, a highly controversial piece of popular culture like *Dallas*. To do this they will have to call on socially available ideologies and images, which channel the way in which such a television serial attains its meanings. It is by tracing these ideologies and images in the letters that we can get to know something about what experiencing pleasure (or otherwise) from *Dallas* implies for these writers – what textual characteristics of *Dallas* organize that experience and in which ideological context it acquires social and cultural meanings. If one general theme is central in this book, then it is the relation between pleasure and ideology.

But it is obvious that this book can never offer an all-embracing unravelling of that relation. There are many ways of enjoying *Dallas*, based on various understandings of what *Dallas* is all about, but only a few ways will be dealt with here – not last because I will be limiting myself to the evidence that can be traced in the relatively small number of letters.

Moreover, any study always bears the traces of the subjectivity of the researcher. Doubtless for that reason my own ambivalent relation to *Dallas* will also have its repercussions. This ambivalence is on the one hand connected with my identity as an intellectual and a feminist, and on the other hand with the fact that I have always particularly liked watching soap operas like *Dallas*. At one time I really belonged to the category of devoted *Dallas* fans. The admission of the reality of this pleasure also formed the starting point for this study – I wanted in the first place to understand this pleasure, without having to pass judgement on whether *Dallas* is good or bad, from a political, social or aesthetic view. Quite the contrary; in my opinion it is important to emphasize how difficult it is to make such judgements – and hence to try to formulate the terms for a progressive cultural politics – when pleasure is at stake. 'Any research is a sort of autobiography', as the anthropologist Georges Dévereux once said. It is for others to judge whether the analyses and arguments presented here are also recognizable and convincing in a more general sense.

1

DALLAS
between reality and fiction

Manipulation or fascination?

Some of the letter-writers dislike *Dallas*, others find it amusing to watch – at least that is what they say. 'Hating *Dallas*' or 'loving *Dallas*' are only labels people stick on the way in which they relate in general to the programme. These are names for the way in which they experience the programme – an experience which can go either in a negative or in a positive direction. But what is hidden behind those apparently unambiguous labels? In fact no single experience, certainly no experience of something as complex as a long-running television serial, is unambiguous: it is always ambivalent and contradictory. The 'totalizing' labels of love and hate conceal this. It is not therefore surprising that in various letters passages can be found in which ambivalences come to the surface – mostly implicit, but sometimes quite explicit, such as in these extracts:

pleasant or not, you are curious as to what is happening to them. For me it is a cosy and sometimes exciting half hour (or how long does it last?) though sometimes I get really annoyed. (Letter 11)

When I saw *Dallas* for the first time I found it a very amusing serial and decided to follow it. But after a few months it became so tedious that I didn't find it at all interesting any more. But three weeks ago I just happened to watch it once and now I just have to watch it, however boring I find it. It's strange because I don't like watching TV much and so I find this really ridiculous. (Letter 27)

These ambivalent feelings must make us realize that it is difficult to determine what the letter-writers really think of *Dallas*. Indeed, the search for a total and definitive explanation for the way in which different groups of viewers experience the programme would seem to be particularly frustrating because at a certain moment we have to acknowledge that we are chasing an illusion: such an all-embracing explanation is a rationalistic fiction. We must keep this in mind when interpreting the statements of the letter-writers. What they say about *Dallas* is no more than a snapshot of their reception of the programme, an attempt to put a diffuse viewing experience into words. And when something is put into words there are always things which remain unexpressed and implicit.

Nevertheless, one thing is certain. Not a single letter-writer is indifferent to *Dallas*. And they all watch it. How otherwise could they give such detailed descriptions of it? In particular for those who regard themselves as *Dallas*-haters, this is an awkward absurdity. Letter-writer 31, for example, who describes herself as an ardent opponent of *Dallas*, nevertheless betrays intense involvement in the vicissitudes of the Ewings. In great detail she describes everything which in her opinion is wrong with the *Dallas* characters, but paradoxically she even fantasizes on possibilities for their future life. 'But who knows, perhaps Pamela will start an extramarital affair (I must admit she's really beautiful); that would be something to smack your lips over' (Letter 31).

It is as though the attraction of *Dallas* is running counter to her self-declared hatred. How can we explain this contradiction? Is she perhaps being manipulated by the swanky advertising business surrounding *Dallas*? She herself explicitly refers to this:

> In England, where I was in the summer, there was an absolute craze. Besides badges, mugs, spoons, handkerchiefs, teatowels, T-shirts, tablecloths, etc. of Charles and Diana, you could also buy this stuff with J.R.'s head on and 'I love J.R.' or 'I hate J.R.' written on it. I nearly bought a badge with the latter on but I realized that I had nearly got caught in the *Dallas* net. (Letter 31)

It is true: the commercial machinery that has to sell *Dallas* is going full blast. In the Netherlands too, week after week the popular press writes about the ups and downs of the *Dallas* stars. *Dallas* books are on sale everywhere. And there is even a special monthly *Dallas* strip cartoon. But hadn't this letter-writer already been 'caught in the *Dallas* net', even without coming into contact with the J.R. badges? Is it not really the case that watching *Dallas* itself has caught her (in an unpleasant way), in spite of the resistance arising from her commitment to the ideology of mass culture?[1]

It would be naïve to suppose that the marketing practices of the commercial culture industry have no effect whatever on the involvement of the viewers. How great and what that effect is cannot be established here, however. On the other hand it would be far too easy to ascribe the popularity of *Dallas* totally to advertising. We must make a distinction between the programme itself as it can be seen week by week on television, and the advertising practices surrounding it. One letter-writer, who says that she likes *Dallas*, writes the following:

> I had read quite a lot about *Dallas* in *Privé*, *Story* and other such magazines.[2] In America millions watch it, and that wasn't expected over here. In short, an awful amount of fuss

was made of it. In America there were 'J.R. hats', stickers, buttons, posters, etc. And that seemed to me terribly over-done. I don't know if you ever read gossip magazines, but if you do you know how it is. If you cut your finger, you put a plaster on it, and that's that. If Larry Hagman or Linda Gray cut a finger, there are great headlines: 'J.R. (or Sue Ellen) temporarily laid up' or something like that.

Altogether *Dallas* didn't interest me much at first, and when the serial began I didn't watch it. From my colleagues and other girl friends I did hear that it was amusing, but people tend to say that easily. So for quite a time I didn't watch it. When it had been going for about half a year, one of my colleagues suddenly said to me (the day after a *Dallas* episode): 'Hey, you really must watch *Dallas*, it's really fantastic.' She is not the type to fall under the influence of a serial either, so when she said that it had to be worth the effort. (Letter 20)

After that, as she recounted, she was done for: after she had seen the programme once, she didn't miss a week. A tall story, perhaps too tall. But in any case it makes us aware that the advertising of one's own social group can be more effective than that of the popular press. The popular press can perhaps fasten the attention of (potential) viewers on the existence of a programme or arouse curiosity for it, but it is improbable that it can have a straightforward and direct influence on the way in which *viewing* a programme is experienced.[3] As one letter-writer says: 'The women are really as beautiful as the gossip magazines say they are and they have one simple recipe for it. But that's not the point here' (Letter 7).

Relatively independent of the competing discourses revolving around *Dallas* – in the popular press, in advertising, but also by television critics, journalists and other intellectuals – the programme has made its way into the experiential worlds of millions of viewers. There's no doubt the programme does exercise a certain fascination. Against the background of prevalent notions of 'good television', this fascination is itself an ambivalent experience: 'I find the quality rather bad *but* it does have a certain attraction' (Letter 26, my italics). This attraction appears to elude rational explanation. The pleasure of *Dallas* is presented here as something incomprehensible and against the grain: this is a case of what the German sociologist Dieter Prokop has called 'the *nevertheless* fascinating'.[4] In other words, the pleasure of *Dallas* seems to be an enigma.

In this chapter and the next I want to try to unravel something of this enigma. But I do not claim to solve it fully – that would conflict with my conviction that an all-embracing explanation of the way in which viewers experience *Dallas* is impossible. Instead, I want to use as a starting point the statements the letter-writers who say they like *Dallas* make about their attitude to the programme. For these statements reveal, albeit obliquely, something about the way in which *Dallas* is received by *these* viewers. I shall try to interpret these statements and I shall indicate how they link up with the pleasure these viewers experience from *Dallas*. But first it is necessary to explain the theoretical perspective on the basis of which I shall be tackling the problem of pleasure.

Consumption, use-value and pleasure

Placing emphasis on the *pleasure* that people experience from *Dallas* is not a harmless theoretical (and political) choice. By so doing we are acknowledging that people can have a positive relationship with *Dallas* – a hedonistic attitude which is at odds with the doctrine that mass culture primarily manipulates the masses. According to Adorno and Horkheimer, for example, the experience of pleasure in mass culture is a false kind of pleasure, even part of the trick of manipulating the masses more effectively in order to lock them in the eternal status quo of exploitation and oppression. 'Marxists, in particular, have interpreted the fact that people *enjoy* mass culture as a reason for gloom', Simon Frith[5] asserts in his book on rock music. Stuart Hall even talks of the stubborn refusal of the left to consider pleasure. 'The project of the left is directed at the future, at the socialism that has still to come, and that is at odds with the direct experience of pleasure here and now. That causes all sorts of mental blocks when theorizing about the problem.'[6]

Put simply, the current Marxist idea is as follows: because the production of culture is subject to the laws of the capitalist economy, cultural products are degraded into commodities to make as much profit as possible on the market. The exchange value of those products is therefore essential for the producers, leading to a neglect of quality. The capitalist market economy is only interested in the production of surplus value and as such is indifferent to the specific characteristics of the goods: caring only that they are sold and consumed. Mass culture is the extreme embodiment of the subjection of culture to the economy; its most important characteristic is that it provides profit for the producers.

But this is a one-sided presentation of the case. Marx himself stated that 'a commodity only has exchange value in so far as it is at the same time a use-value, i.e., as an object of consumption; it ceases to have an exchange value if it ceases to have a use-value.'[7] In other words, one cannot succeed in selling a commodity if it does not have a certain usefulness. And it is here that the contradictory character of the capitalist mode of production lies. From the standpoint of production the product only features as a commodity, but from the standpoint of consumption the same product features as use-value.

The way in which a cultural product is consumed can therefore not be directly deduced from the way in which it is produced; it is also dependent on all sorts of socio-cultural and psychological conditions. Terry Lovell has explained in a simple and clear way how unmanageable the relation between the commercial and the entertainment value of mass culture can be: 'There will be no guarantee that the use-value of the cultural object for its purchaser will even be compatible with its utility to capitalism as bourgeois ideology [. . .] For example, the utility of a television programme for a producer who buys advertising time is the ability of that programme to enhance the sale of the advertised product, by giving the producer access to the audience which is watching the programme. But the viewer will be watching the programme for its entertainment value and there is some evidence that these two interests may conflict. A programme which is a best seller and which its audience rates very highly on entertainment value may actually be less effective as a vehicle for impressing advertised products and increasing their sales than a less entertaining programme.'[8]

But what is the entertainment value that Lovell is discussing here? Both in common sense and in more theoretical ways of thinking, entertainment is usually associated with simple, un-complicated pleasure – hence the phrase, for example, '*mere* entertainment'. This is to evade the obligation to investigate which mechanisms lie at the basis of that pleasure, how that pleasure is produced and how it works – as though that pleasure were something natural and automatic. Nothing is less true, however. Any form of pleasure is constructed and functions in a specific social and historical context.

How then is the pleasure of *Dallas* constructed? As a product of the commercial culture industry, *Dallas* is explicitly offered to the public as an object for pleasurable consumption. The promise of pleasure is the use-value by which the industry tries to seduce viewers to watch *Dallas* on their television sets. But to achieve this aim the producers have to have a definite idea of what the audience will find pleasurable; they must have a certain self-confidence that their own definition of pleasure will coincide with that of (large sections of) the public. There-fore the strategy of the producers will be directed at the elaboration of what they already know about popular pleasures. Their previous experience in the business will be of assistance to them in this. Hence it is not very likely that the pleasure offered in *Dallas* will be structurally new, ex-perimental or provocative. It will keep within the guidelines of existing and accepted definitions and routines of popular pleasure. In order to attract a large audience the format of *Dallas* will therefore tend to accord with easily accessible and current patterns of what is pleasurable and entertaining. This does not, however, mean that the producers will be fully aware of the effectiveness of their product. As a matter of fact, it is only necessary for them to know that the mechanisms *work* – something they try to discover, for example, by audience ratings and programme testing – not *how* and *why* they work. From their pragmatic viewpoint they are not interested in cultural theory.

We, however, do wish to know how and why the mechanisms of pleasure function – we have indeed set ourselves the task, if not to solve the riddle of the pleasure of *Dallas*, then at least to unravel it to some degree. In 'The aristocracy of culture',[9] Pierre Bourdieu has explained that popular pleasure is characterized by an immediate emotional or sensual involvement in the object of pleasure. What matters is the possibility of identifying oneself with it in some way or other, to integrate it into everyday life. In other words, popular pleasure is first and foremost a pleasure of recognition. But what do *Dallas*-lovers recognize in *Dallas*? This is now the main question confronting us.

DALLAS as television entertainment

But is it really possible to isolate pleasure in *Dallas* from pleasure in television in general? Could it not be said that pleasure in *Dallas* is connected not so much with the specific characteristics of the programme itself, as with the pleasure of watching television as such? And would it not be nearer the truth to say that the audience watches *Dallas* because it has little choice, because television just is not offering anything better?

The consumption of *Dallas* is not an isolated phenomenon, but is embedded in a network of other activities and associations which are connected with those activities. We should not inflate the pleasure in *Dallas* into something unique and therefore elusive. We have to take into account the socio-cultural context in which *Dallas* is consumed. These conditions of consumption are of course not the same for all social categories and groups. Quite the contrary – an enquiry into the *different* ways in which the television serial is received by various population groups and subcultures could in fact yield particularly useful insights and apply a corrective to the prevalent image of 'passive consumption'.[10] But this would demand a wide-scale sociological examination and that is not my intention. Instead I will confine myself here to describing some general socio-cultural and ideological conditions of television viewing.

For the great majority of the population, television viewing is associated with entertainment: it means relaxation, resting after the day's work. Entertainment belongs to the domain of leisure, and leisure is regarded in the everyday experiential world as 'time for yourself', as liberation from the chafing bonds of the official world of factory, school or office, or from the worries of running the home.[11] Entertainment has for most people expressly positive associations; it is seen as a right, as something earned. And if one thing is associated with watching television as a cultural practice, then it is the right to be entertained in one's own living room. The fact then that *Dallas* is presented as an entertainment programme already offers the promise of pleasure. No one will regard watching *Dallas* as an irksome duty.[12] One letter-writer described it like this: 'a programme it's nice to sit/lie watching, intellect set at nil, the rare luxury of doing sweet nothing' (Letter 19). And another letter-writer gives the following reason why she watches it: 'It's a "penny dreadful" but relaxing. You don't have to strain yourself to understand the story. Just the thing after a hard day's work' (Letter 42).

Pleasure in *Dallas* is therefore associated with the pleasure of the freedoms of entertainment, in which people feel released from the prohibitions and demands of society. Although many leisure practices are organized socially, in the day-to-day reality leisure time is experienced as an enclave to which one can retreat, 'be oneself'. And in this the weekend occupies a special place; it has the most pleasant associations. 'I just find it a pity that it isn't on Friday any more, because I found that a really good evening for it. But never mind, I'll still watch it on Tuesdays. This evening I'll be sitting there ready and waiting at half past nine' (Letter 2).

But why does it have to be *Dallas*? Isn't this programme just one of many entertainment programmes and is not its pleasure merely something fortuitous? There are three lines of argument which seem to suggest that the popularity of *Dallas* derives not so much from its own qualities as from the fact that it is a *television* programme.

In the first place, *Dallas* is usually televised at prime time. If in addition the other television channels are broadcasting few attractive popular programmes (which has certainly been the case in the Netherlands for a season)[13] it is not surprising that large groups of viewers set to watching *Dallas* – apparently just because they want to watch television, not because they are particularly interested in it. Of course this situation will have a positive influence on the *size* of the audience. But in spite of that it cannot explain the extremely high viewing figures attained by *Dallas* (which are only a quantitative indication of the popularity of the programme anyway).

The second argument points to the nature of television viewing as such. According to Raymond Williams watching television is strongly influenced by the 'flow' character of programming: a coming and going of programmes without their individuality leaving any especially deep impression, because there is no time. Before one programme has finished, another has begun. '[M]ost of us say, in describing the experience, that we have been "watching television", rather than that we have watched "the news" or "a play" or "the football on television". Certainly we sometimes say both, but the fact that we say the former at all is already significant', Williams states.[14] Formally speaking, then, our contact with particular programmes is shortlived, casual and superficial. Furthermore, television viewing is one of the most obvious and easy-to-realize forms of leisure activity: because the television set is permanently available – it nearly always occupies a central place in the living room – television viewing has almost become an extension of daily life and routine activity. All these socio-cultural characteristics of television viewing as such do indeed set limits on the unique nature of watching *Dallas*. But that does not mean that the programme does not occupy a special place within those limits: the very fact that so much has been said and written about it proves that *Dallas* plays a prominent role in the cultural consciousness of society (at least for the time being: even popular pleasures are subject to fashion to a large degree).

Finally, there is yet a third argument about why we cannot just take the pleasure of *Dallas* on its own terms. This has to do with the authoritarian character of television programming: it is the television networks which decide which programmes are to be broadcast and which not. The audience can only wait and see what menu it will be served. In this sense the television audience is 'passive'. It could then be reasoned that people watch *Dallas* for lack of anything better. But the remarkable thing about television programming, certainly that of commercially run networks, is that it is dominated by the idea of 'giving the public what it wants'.[15] This self-image of the television network is of great influence in the selection of programmes to be broadcast. Certainly where entertainment programmes are concerned there is no doubt that those programmes are selected which are *thought* likely to take the fancy of the public at large. Of course such a programming policy does run the risk that the law of the 'greatest common denominator' will come to prevail. On the other hand, however, ironically enough, this strategy also has the advantage that it does have to take account of the general wishes and preferences of the public. A commercial television network, from the point of view of its own economic logic, cannot allow itself to become paternalistic; quite the contrary, a populist attitude belongs as it were 'spontaneously' to the professional ideology of the commercial culture industry. It is therefore undeniable that the principles of commercialism do tend to lead to serious considerations of (some of) the wishes of the audience. The fact that the preferences and feelings of the audience are capricious and unpredictable explains why the culture industry feels the need to put so much money and energy into market research – although the motives for this are dubious, being purely pragmatic and egoistic. In short, to use Frith's words, '"giving the public what it wants", the classic huckster's phrase, describes in fact a complicated relationship between "supply" and "demand"'.[16]

The audience itself didn't ask for *Dallas*: it got it 'thrown into its lap', as it were, as a present from a distant uncle in America. But once it had got it, it then started 'playing' with that present – it was clearly happy with it, happier than with most other 'presents' offered by television. This manifest preference of the audience is certainly limited by the range of what is on offer, but this does not necessarily mean that *Dallas* is consumed in a passive and resigned way. In fact, viewers put a lot of emotional energy into it and experience pleasure from it. Once again, then, the question of pleasure confronts us.

DALLAS as text

In reading the letters we encounter an avalanche of self-given 'reasons' why lovers of *Dallas* like watching the programme. The letter-writers extensively describe their viewing experiences and state what does and does not appeal to them.

> I find *Dallas* a super TV programme. For me it means relaxation twice a week, out of the daily rut. You may wonder why twice a week – well, that's because I watch it on

Belgian TV too. You have to switch over, but you quickly pick it up again. I'm interested in the clothes, make-up and hair-dos too. Sometimes it's quite gripping too, for example in Miss Ellie's case. [. . .] And I think Ray Krebbs is wonderful. But I think J.R. is a monster, a hypocrite, etc. (Letter 1)

The reason I like watching it is that you can easily get really involved in their problems. Yet all the time you know it will all turn out all right again. In fact it's a flight from reality. (Letter 5)

Why do I watch *Dallas* every Tuesday? Mainly because of Pamela and that wonderful love between her and Bobby. When I see those two I feel warmth radiating from them. I am happily married myself too and perhaps I see myself in Pamela. I find her very beautiful too (which I myself am not). (Letter 8)

First of all it's entertainment for me, part show, expensive clothes, beautiful horses, something I can just do with by the evening. (Letter 11)

I think it's marvellous to project myself into *Dallas* and in my mind to give J.R. a good hiding when he's just pulled off yet another dirty trick, or admire Miss Ellie because she always tries to see the best in everyone or to bring it out in them. (Letter 13)

I find *Dallas* marvellous, though it isn't an absolute 'must' for me. Reasons:
Everyone is so kind to one another (leaving aside J.R.) and they form a real family, being sociable, having their meals together, for example.
Witty dialogue.
Fast, characteristic of an American product. (Letter 17)

My absorption in *Dallas* has to do with the fact that I follow everything coming from America. I have been there once – last year – and I started watching *Dallas* just to see the American city scene: those beautiful apartment blocks (especially the really beautiful one you see during the titles) and the cars. (Letter 21)

I don't find everything entertaining. The farm doesn't interest me much. Now and then you get a whole episode with nothing but cowboys and cattle. I find that boring, I'm not keen on Westerns. Too macho. Like the episode when the Ewing men went hunting and were chased. Boring. After that it got better again, fortunately. [. . .] I like the pictures of the city too a lot. The office buildings in Dallas. The talks about oil. I really enjoy that. (Letter 23; this letter is from a man)

I find the situations always so well chosen and excellently fitting together and everything runs so well from one thing into another. Then I find the milieu (a rich oil family, etc.) very well chosen. (Letter 40, also from a man)

It is clear that there is not just one 'reason' for the pleasure of *Dallas*, which applies for everyone; each has his or her own more or less unique relationship to the programme. What appeals to us in such a television serial is connected with our individual life histories, with the social situation we are in, with the aesthetic and cultural preferences we have developed, and so on.

But though the ideas of each of the letter-writers are of course personal, they cannot be regarded as a direct expression of their 'motives' or 'reasons' for watching *Dallas*. They can at most be regarded as indications or symptoms of deeper psychological incentives and orientations. Furthermore, although these ideas can *appear* to be strictly personal for the letter-writers themselves, ultimately all these ideas are structured in a specific socio-cultural manner. And so we must take a look behind these ideas; we must subject them to a 'symptomatic reading' to be able to say something about the pleasure of *Dallas* that rises above the merely individual level.

It would be going too far to say that viewers are completely free to handle *Dallas* as they want, as the possibilities of experiencing pleasure in it are not infinite. *Dallas* itself, as an object of pleasure, sets its own limits on those possibilities. From the letter excerpts I have just quoted it emerges that the ideas expressed by these viewers contain many elements referring to what is to be seen in the programme – to its textual characteristics. This fact makes it necessary to go into the specific way in which *Dallas*, as a cultural object, is structured.

Dallas is a weekly television programme. A television programme consists of a series of electronic images and sounds which emerge from a television set. These images and sounds represent something: people talking, walking, drinking, high-rise apartment blocks, moving cars, and so on. From this standpoint a television programme can be looked on as a *text*: as a system of representation consisting of a specific combination of (visual and audible) signs.[17] The problem here, however, is that *Dallas* is a discontinuous text: it is a television serial consisting of a large number of episodes, each more or less forming a separate whole. Each episode can then in its turn be called a textual unit. For the sake of clarity I shall view the television serial *Dallas* as a whole as an incomplete, 'infinite' text.[18]

A text functions only if it is 'read'. Only in and through the practice of reading does the text have meaning (or several meanings) for the reader. In the confrontation between *Dallas* and its viewers the reading activity of the latter is therefore the connecting principle. And this reading does not occur just anyhow. As David Morley says: 'The activity of "getting meaning" from [a] message is ... a problematic practice, however transparent and "natural" it may seem.'[19] A reader has to know specific codes and conventions in order to be able to have any grasp of what a text is about. So it is not by any means a matter of course for viewers to know directly that in *Dallas* they are dealing with a fictional text and not, for example, with a documentary. A great deal of cultural knowledge is necessary to be able to recognize a text as fiction. In *Dallas* – as is the custom in all television serials – certain hints are given for this, such as the titles, presenting the actors one after another, the music, etc.

Any text employs certain rhetorical strategies to arouse the interest of the viewers, and obviously *Dallas* succeeds in attracting the attention of millions of people with very varied social, cultural and psychological backgrounds, and maintaining their involvement in the programme. Very general and widespread structural characteristics of television programmes such as *Dallas* contribute to this.

The function of characters

How do viewers get involved in a television serial like *Dallas*, and what does this involvement consist of? The Belgian media theoretician Jean-Marie Piemme, in his book on the television serial genre,[20] asserts that this involvement occurs because viewers are enabled to participate in the 'world' of the serial. This participation does not come of its own accord, but must be *produced*:

> If, in the serial [. . .] participation can be brought about, this is certainly because this activity has psychological foundations, but it is also because these psychological foundations are confronted by a type of discourse allowing them to be activated. In other words, the structure of the discourse which sustains the serial produces the participation as well as the psychological attitude.[21]

The structure of the text itself therefore plays an essential role in stimulating the involvement of viewers. More importantly still, according to Piemme, it is impossible to watch a television serial without some degree of personal involvement. 'To watch a serial', he states, 'is much more than seeing it: it is also involving oneself in it, letting oneself be held in suspense, sharing the feelings of the characters, discussing their psychological motivations and their conduct, deciding whether they are right or wrong, in other words living "their world".'[22] But what is there so particular about the textual structure of television serials that makes them able to effect such profound involvement?

In commonsense explanations of the attraction of television serials, textual structure and its effects are generally ignored. Often single elements of the story are held responsible for the popularity of a serial. Commentary in the press about *Dallas*, for example, shows a special preference for the striking role of the 'baddie' J.R. One of the letter-writers, however, mentions her preference for another *Dallas* character: 'Sue Ellen is definitely my favourite. She has a psychologically believable character. As she is, I am too to a lesser degree ("knocking one's head against a wall once too often") and I want to be (attractive). Identification, then' (Letter 17). But such identification with one character does not take place in a vacuum. One does not just recognize oneself in the ascribed characteristics of an isolated fictional character. That character occupies a specific position within the context of the narrative as a whole: only in relation to other characters in the narrative is her or his 'personality' brought out. In other words, identification with a character only becomes possible within the framework of the whole structure of the narrative.

Moreover, the involvement of viewers cannot be described exclusively in terms of an imaginary identification with one or more characters. Several other aspects of the text contribute to this, such as the way in which the story is told, or the staging. This does not mean, however, that the characters play a subordinate role in the realization of participation. According to Piemme, in a television serial the characters even function as the pre-eminent narrative element which provides the point of impact for the involvement of viewers. But it is not so much the personalities ascribed to the characters in the story, as their formal narrative status that matters. In a fictional text like the television serial the characters are central. Through the characters the various elements of the text (situations, actions, locations, indications of time and so on) obtain a place and function in the plot. Because the viewer imagines the characters as active subjects, those elements are stripped of their arbitrariness and obtain meaning in the narrative. Furthermore, the 'lifelike' acting style ensures that the distance between actor and character is minimized, so that the illusion is created that we are dealing with a 'real person'. The character therefore appears for the viewer as a person existing independently of the narrative situations shown in the serial. The character becomes a person appearing to lead an autonomous life outside the fiction of the serial; she or he becomes a person of flesh and blood, one of us. The popular press regularly plays on this illusion: the names of actors and actresses and those of the characters are often used interchangeably or merged – Larry 'J.R.' Hagman.

Being able to imagine the characters as 'real people' thus forms a necessary precondition for the involvement of viewers and is an anchor for the pleasure of *Dallas*. This theoretical assertion is reflected in the letters. When the letter-writers comment on the characters, it is almost always in the same way as we talk about people in daily life: in terms of character traits. The characters are not so much judged for their position in the *Dallas* narrative, as for *how they are*.

That at least is the case for the letter-writers who like *Dallas*. Those who dislike *Dallas* appear to keep a little more distant from the characters. Some of them even criticize their 'unreal' nature.

> One of them (his name escapes me) is always the bastard with his sneaky ideas and tricks, the other son is the goody together with his wife, J.R.'s wife (found the name now) is always 'sloshed' and going off alone to her room. (Letter 32)

> When they can't think up any more problems they send Digger after Miss Ellie and change Sue Ellen around a bit again, while J.R. (over the top) is well away with Sue Ellen's sister. (Letter 36)

> I find the characters appearing in the serial very caricatured [. . .] J.R. with his crazy ideas: always the same teeth-

gritting. He is also a very caricatured figure, that is obvious.
Oh, how bad he is. It's really laid on thick. I find his wife the
most lifelike figure in the serial. I think because she was in
such a difficult position the writers had most chances with
her. What I really can't stand though is the facial expression
she has on. Has on, I can't call it anything else. It looks as
though her head is cast in plastic. (Letter 41)

What is striking in these reactions is not only a rejection of
the 'personalities' of the *Dallas* people, but also an indignation
over their constructedness. Those who like *Dallas*, on the other
hand, write much more sympathetically about them. In their
descriptions a much greater emotional involvement emerges in
the characters as people, even when they find them unsympathetic. As one fan of *Dallas* writes:

Actually they are all a bit stupid. And oversensational.
Affected and genuinely American. [. . .] And yet [. . .] the
Ewings go through a lot more than I do. They seem to have a
richer emotional life. Everyone knows them in Dallas. Sometimes they run into trouble, but they have a beautiful house
and anything else they might want. (Letter 21)

The personalities of the characters are for some fans
apparently so important that they have spontaneously included a whole list of characterizations and criticisms in their
letters. They make clear to us how central the characters are in
their viewing experience.

I don't know whether it's what you want but I'll write what I
myself think of the characters too.
Miss Ellie: a nice woman.
Jock: mean, doesn't know himself exactly what he wants, I
think.
Bobby: someone who has respect everywhere and for everyone (except for J.R. but that's understandable).
J.R.: Just a bastard. I personally can't stand him but I must
say he plays his role well.

Pamela: a nice girl (I find her a woman of character; she can be nice, but nasty too).

Sue Ellen: has had bad luck with J.R., but she makes up for it by being a flirt. I don't like her much. And she's too sharp-tongued.

Lucy: she has rather too high an opinion of herself, other-wise she's quite nice (she's made up too old).

I don't know so much about the rest who take part in *Dallas* so I won't write about them. If you need what I've said here about these characters then I hope you can use it. If not tear it up. (Letter 3)

Now I'll describe the main characters a little, perhaps that might be useful for you too. Here we go then.

Jock: a well-meaning duffer, rather surly and hard-headed, a very haughty man.

Miss Ellie: very nice, sensitive, understanding, courageous, in other words a real mother.

J.R.: very egoistic, hard as nails, keen on power, but a man with very little heart.

Sue Ellen: just *fantastic*, tremendous how that woman acts, the movements of her mouth, hands, etc. That woman really enters into her role, looking for love, snobbish, in short a real woman.

Pamela: a Barbie doll with no feelings, comes over as false and unsympathetic (a waxen robot).

Bobby: ditto.

Lucy: likeable, naïve, a real adolescent. (Letter 12)

On the characters: Sue Ellen is definitely my favourite. She has a psychologically believable character. [. . .] (Her friend, Dusty, really loves her and for that reason, although the cowboy business in the serial irritates me and so he does too a bit, I do like him as far as I can judge.)

Miss Ellie is all right too. She looks good, always knows the

right thing to do (conciliatory and firm) within the family
and her breast cancer gave her some depth.
Lucy has guts, but is a wicked little sod too.
The others don't offer much as characters, I believe. Pamela
pouts, and is too sweet. I have absolutely nothing to say
about Jock and Bobby; J.R. is really incredible, so mean.
(Letter 17)

What is interesting in these extracts is not so much the
content of the character descriptions (although the difference
in sympathies in itself is worth some attention), but the fact that
'genuineness' forms the basis for evaluation. The more
'genuine' a character appears to be, the more he or she is
valued. But what is even more remarkable is that even for the
severe critics 'genuineness' is the criterion by which they judge
the characters. The only difference is that the severe critics tend
to see them as 'unreal', whereas among the fans the opposite is
the case. Characters who are 'caricatures' or 'improbable' are
not esteemed, characters who are 'lifelike' or 'psychologically
believable' are. Also, casually dropped remarks from fans
quoted above ('I must say he plays his role well', 'she's made up
too old' and 'tremendous how that woman acts, the movements of her mouth, hands, etc.') make clear that these letter-
writers are very well aware that they are only dealing with
fictional 'real people'. Such remarks indicate that these viewers
would like that fictional element eliminated as far as possible.
In their eyes actor and character should merge:

. . . then I find that all the actors and actresses act very well.
So well even that, for example, I really find J.R. a bastard, or
Sue Ellen a frustrated lady. (Letter 18)

. . . Because in my opinion they have chosen awfully good
actors. I mean suitable for the role they are playing. The
whole Ewing family is played so well that they are really
human. Sometimes you get a film or a play and you think:
God, if I really had to do that, I'd react quite differently.
Then it seems so unreal. But usually *Dallas* could really

happen, and the actors and actresses make it credible. (Letter 20)

The people taking part in it act terribly well. (Letter 4)

The effect of 'genuineness' is then the most important thing these viewers expect. Only when they experience the fiction of the serial as 'genuine' can they feel involved in it. They have to be able to believe that the characters constructed in the text are 'real people' whom they can find pleasant or unpleasant, with whom they can feel affinity or otherwise, and so on. It could be said that such involvement is a necessary condition for the pleasure of *Dallas*.

The (un)realistic quality of DALLAS

But genuine-seeming *people* alone are not enough. According to Piemme, the fictional *world* in which the characters live must seem equally real. But how 'real' or 'realistic' is this world? This rather vague concept of 'realism' also seems to play an important part in the letters. 'Realism' seems to be a favourite criterion among viewers for passing judgement on *Dallas*. And here 'realistic' is always associated with 'good' and 'unrealistic' with 'bad'. So it is not surprising that many haters of *Dallas* express their dislike by referring to its – in their opinion – 'unrealistic' content. Here are some letter extracts:

In *Dallas* no attention at all is paid to any realistic problems in this world. The problems of ordinary people. (Letter 31)

. . . in my eyes the characters appearing in it are totally unreal. (Letter 38)

It is a programme situated pretty far outside reality. The mere fact that a whole family is living in one house comes over as rather unreal. What happens in this serial you would never run into in the street or in your circle of acquaintance: very unreal events. The family relations that are so weirdly involved: this one's married to the sister of the enemy of his brother, etc., etc. (Letter 41)

1. It is an improbable story because:
    1.1 Such a rich family would scarcely live as three families in one house (at least in a Western society), so that privacy for each family is minimal:
        1.1.1 They breakfast together, etc.
        1.1.2 Other than the common rooms each family only has one bedroom (no separate sitting room or study, etc.).
        1.1.3 The whole family concerns itself with everything.
    1.2 Too much happens in the short time and then it's all dramatic situations, not only for the main characters, but for the minor characters as well. This latter makes things confusing.
    1.3 The actors are rather clichéd types, i.e. they keep up a certain role or attitude. Normal people are more complex.
2. Thanks to the constant drama there is a certain tension in the story, but this is exaggerated. Even in a more realistic story there can be tension and I actually find that nicer. (Letter 42)

In these extracts a number of things are striking. In the first place these letter-writers find *Dallas* 'unrealistic' because in their opinion the world and the events in the story do not coincide with the world and events outside *Dallas*: reality 'as it is'. A text is called 'realistic' here if the 'reality' standing outside and independent of the text is reflected in an 'adequate' way. But – and this is the second striking point – the letter-writers each invest the notion of 'reality' with a different content. For some the represented reality must coincide with the social reality of 'ordinary people' (i.e. 'real' problems such as unemployment and housing shortages and not the 'mock problems' of the rich); for others that reality must be 'recognizable', i.e. comparable to one's own environment; and for others again the world presented must be 'probable', i.e. cohere, be 'normal'. Finally, a text is also occasionally called 'unrealistic' if people find that it simplifies the 'real' reality (whatever that may be), exaggerates it or reflects it in clichés.

As we can see, the significance of the notion '(un)realistic' can assume different forms. Clearly there is no unambiguous definition of what 'realism' contains. But in the way in which the term is used by the letter-writers quoted, at least an essential community of ideas can be discerned: they all call *Dallas* 'unrealistic' because in their opinion it gives a 'distorted image of reality'. This definition of realism, in which a comparison of the realities 'in' and 'outside' a text is central, we can call 'empiricist realism'.[23] This empiricist concept of realism often fulfils an ideological function in television criticism in so far as its standards are used to furnish arguments for criticizing programmes and to strengthen the concept itself. From this point of view, a text which can be seen as an 'unrealistic' rendering of social reality (however that is defined) is 'bad'. And as we have seen, *Dallas* is often subjected to this judgement.

But having said this, we are immediately confronted by an apparently baffling contradiction. Contrary to the critics and those who dislike *Dallas*, who regard it as particularly 'unrealistic', many fans do find it 'realistic'. Some letter-writers even see the – in their eyes – realistic content of *Dallas* as a reason for the pleasure they experience.

> I find *Dallas* super and for this reason: they reflect the daily life of a family (I find). (Letter 3)

> It is realistic (for me anyway), other people think I'm mad, things happen in it we might well find happening to us later (or have had). (Letter 12)

How should we interpret this contradiction? Should we ascribe to these letter-writers a 'false consciousness' because their judgement on the 'realistic' content of *Dallas* is totally wrong?

Or is there more to it? Reasoning from an empiricist-realistic standpoint, we can simply say these letter-writers are misled. In *Dallas*, according to this reasoning, the 'daily life of a family' is certainly not being reflected – for, as one letter-writer suggests: 'I wonder why these people in Heaven's name carry on living in the same house!' (Letter 36). Furthermore, it could be said that the things that happen in it are certainly not things 'we might well find happening to us', for it is clear that in *Dallas* there is an improbable accumulation of sensational events, such as airplane accidents, weird diseases, kidnappings, etc. In short, if *Dallas* is regarded as a mirror of 'the' reality, then we should recognize that it is a big distorting mirror, or more seriously, 'a twisted image of reality'.

But this empiricist conception of realism presents problems for a number of reasons. I shall cite two difficulties here. First, it is wrongly based on the assumption – and this is inherent in empiricism – that a text *can* be a direct, immediate reproduction or reflection of an 'outside world'. This is to ignore the fact that everything that is processed in a text is the result of selection and adaptation: elements of the 'real world' function only as raw material for the production process of texts. The empiricist conception denies the fact that each text is a cultural product realized under specific ideological and social conditions of production. And so there can never be any question of an unproblematic mirror relation between text and social reality: at most it can be said that a text constructs its own version of 'the real'. As Raymond Williams says: 'The most damaging consequence of any theory of art as reflection is that [. . .] it succeeds in suppressing the actual work on material [. . .] which is the making of any art work.'[24]

The second difficulty is connected with this. The empiricist conception of realism cannot do justice to the fact that a large number of *Dallas* fans do seem to *experience* it as 'realistic'. Must we regard this experience merely as the result of incorrect reading and must we, consequently, accuse the letter-writers who read 'wrongly' of a lack of knowledge of reality? It is, to say the least, unsatisfactory just to dismiss this very prevalent way of responding to the programme. A more structural explanation must be possible.

DALLAS and the realistic illusion

In the empiricist conception of realism the thematic content of the narrative becomes the guideline for the assessment of the 'realistic' nature of the text. Some literary and film theoreticians on the other hand make the way in which the story is told responsible for what is called the 'realistic illusion': the illusion that a text is a faithful reflection of an actually existing world emerges as a result of the fact that the constructedness of the text is suppressed. Piemme states that it is this suppression which fosters the involvement of viewers in the serial: 'Participation can only function by denying itself as product of discourse. What produces it must suppress the marks of its production in order that the illusion of the natural, the spontaneous, the inevitable, may function.'[25] In other words, the realistic illusion is not something to be blamed on the ignorance or lack of knowledge of the viewers, but is generated by the formal structure of the text itself; the thematic content plays only a subordinate role here.

The film theoretician Colin MacCabe calls a (literary or film) text which arouses such a realistic illusion a 'classic realistic text'.[26] Characteristic of such a text, for which the nineteenth-century realistic novel is the model, is the dominant role which the story in itself plays.[27] It is told in such a way that the viewer or reader is unaware that the narrative has a narrator. In a classic realistic text 'narrative must deny the time of its own telling – it must refuse its status as discourse [. . .] in favour of its self-presentation as simple identity, complete knowledge'.[28] In short, the classic realistic text conceals its own status as narrative and acts as though the story 'speaks for itself'.

With regard to film, in this connection the term 'transparent narrative cinema' is used: 'transparent' because the screen appears to be a transparent window on the events taking place in the film story. The classic-realistic method of narration is the most common in the history of the cinema, but it is mainly in classical Hollywood that the conventions of transparent narrativity have been perfected to the utmost. What then are these conventions?[29]

A Hollywood-story is always about individual characters who want or desire something. The characters perform actions to achieve their goals, but can encounter opposition to this from other characters who have other wishes or desires. From this schema flows a chain of events which are in a cause/effect relationship with one another. This chain forms the framework of the story.

This story must be told filmically, i.e. translated into a concrete sequence of images and sounds. Countless technical and aesthetic means are necessary to translate an abstract narrative into a concrete film story: the narrative must be divided into scenes, the sequence of the scenes and shots determined, locations must be sought, actors selected and their acting style defined, the camera must focus the *mise-en-scène* in a specific way and the individual shots must finally be assembled together. It is characteristic of a transparent narrative film that all these filmic operations are made subordinate to the demands of the story. Everything we see or hear in the film has a narrative function: 'meaningless' images and sounds are deemed redundant and tend to be excluded. Through this the illusion arises that the story is unrolling before our eyes without any mediation: the narrating instance has been effectively eliminated.

In Hollywood since the beginning of this century certain iron rules of cinematography have been developed (such as continuity editing, classic montage, etc.) to create this suggestion of narrative spontaneity. But we no longer experience these rules as rules, because we have become so used to this dominant American film language that we no longer even recognize it as a language. This is the socio-cultural background of the realistic illusion.

The television serial *Dallas* also uses the classical Hollywood rules to a great degree. The story concerns the members of the Ewing family: it is their desires and wishes that propel the narrative, their actions (and the mutual conflicts they have as a result of these) fill the narrative. The whole construction of the serial is also directed at showing those actions and their consequences. All the elements in the film are at the service of the narrative. Because the narrative wants the characters to be rich a beautiful ranch is chosen as their house, they drive luxury cars and the women wear expensive clothes. And the camera only portrays what is necessary for understanding the story: where something is happening, there stands the camera. A scene is broken off the moment the dramatic action in it has come to an end: there is no point in remaining at that place any longer. Moreover, the successive scenes run smoothly into one another: jumps in time and space must take place in such a way that the viewer does not find them disturbing, for this can lead to a loss of illusion of narrative continuity and coherence. This illusion is strengthened even more by the strictly chronological sequence in which the course of the narrative is set forth; what first happens in the story we get to see before later events. (The only exception to this is the 'flashback', which is, however, announced so explicitly as a retrospection of one of the characters that no misunderstandings can arise over it.)

According to MacCabe and others[30] it is precisely this constructed illusion of reality which is the basis for pleasure. It is pleasurable to be able to deny the textuality and the fictional nature of the film and forget it: it gives the viewers a comfortable and cosy feeling because they can 'let the narrative flow over them' without any effort. The apparent 'transparency' of the narrative produces a feeling of direct involvement, because it ensures that the viewer can act exactly *as though* the story really happened. In other words, according to this theory pleasure in *Dallas* could be regarded as a pleasure in the obvious, apparently natural meaningfulness of the ups and downs of the Ewing family and the people around them. It is the *form* of the narrative which produces pleasure, not its content.

Yet this explanation of pleasure is not totally satisfactory, precisely because it abstracts from the concrete narrative-content.[31] Transparent narrativity alone is not enough to get pleasure out of a text; not all transparent narrative texts are experienced as equally pleasurable. On the contrary, the thematic differences between such texts are of interest, as one of the letter-writers states: 'For me *Dallas* is comparable to *Dynasty*. Other American series (*Magnum, Hulk, Charlie's Angels, Starsky and Hutch*, in short, violence) I can appreciate less' (Letter 17). Thus the pleasure of *Dallas* is not only to do with the illusion of reality which is produced by its transparent narrativity – although it might be said that this illusion is a general condition of pleasure as it is experienced by a lot of viewers. *What* is told in the narrative must also play a part in the production of pleasure.

DALLAS and 'emotional realism'

Why then do so many fans call *Dallas* 'realistic'? What do they recognize as 'real' in its fictional world?

A text can be read at various levels. The first level is the literal, denotative level. This concerns the literal, manifest content of the *Dallas* narrative: the discussions between the characters, their actions, their reactions to one another, and so on. Is this literal content of the *Dallas* story experienced as realistic by viewers? It does not look like it. Indeed, we can say that the above-quoted letter-writers who dislike *Dallas* are talking on this literal narrative-level when they dismiss the programme as *un*realistic. Let us repeat a letter extract:

It is a programme situated pretty far outside reality. The mere fact that a whole family is living in one house comes over as rather unreal. What happens in this serial you would never run into in the street or in your circle of acquaintance: very unreal events. The family relationships that are so weirdly involved: this one's married to the sister of the enemy of his brother, etc., etc. (Letter 41)

This indicates that the *Dallas* narrative at the level of denotation is not exactly regarded as realistic; literal resemblances are scarcely seen between the fictional world as it is constructed in *Dallas* and the 'real' world. Again the inadequacy of the empiricist-realistic approach becomes clear here. It is only sensitive to the denotative level of the narrative. Therefore it can only see the fact that so many *Dallas* fans obviously do experience the programme as realistic as a paradox.

A text can, however, also be read at another level, namely at the connotative level.[32] This level relates to the associative meanings which can be attributed to elements of the text. The same letter-writer we have just quoted also wrote the following: 'The nice thing about the serial is that it has a semblance of humanity, it is not so unreal that you can't relate to it any more. There are recognizable things, recognizable people, recognizable relations and situations in it' (Letter 41).

It is striking; the same things, people, relations and situations which are regarded at the denotative level as unrealistic, and unreal, are at connotative level apparently not seen at all as unreal, but in fact as 'recognizable'. Clearly, in the connotative reading process the denotative level of the text is put in brackets.

But what does make *Dallas* so 'recognizable' at that connotative level? What does that 'semblance of humanity' consist of that this letter-writer is talking about?

In the letters we come across all kinds of descriptions which can give us some indication of the associative meanings these viewers ascribe to *Dallas*. From the heterogeneous stream of signs with which viewers are confronted when they watch the television serial, they pick up only certain things; they find only certain elements of the whole text relevant, striking – pleasurable. In other words, a text is never read in its totality; during reading a selection process is always taking place. As Roland Barthes has noted in *The Pleasure of the Text*, 'it is the very rhythm of what is read and what is not read that creates the pleasure of the great narratives. [. . .] Thus, what I enjoy in a narrative is not directly its content or even its structure, but rather the abrasions I impose upon the fine surface: I read on, I skip, I look up, I dip again.'[33] In a similar way, we could say that the letter-writers only name those elements from *Dallas* which are important for them in some way or other, which for them make up the special and pleasurable quality of *Dallas*.[34]

Many lovers of *Dallas* say that they find it pleasurable because it is 'realistic'. From their letters we can now get an impression of how they reach that judgement, or more precisely, which elements of the text they select which lead to its 'realism' at a connotative level. Note the similarity between the meanings which emerge in the following letter extracts.

> I find *Dallas* super and for this reason: [the characters] reflect the daily life of a family (I find). You sometimes see serials where everything runs smoothly. Never any rows or anything. Not a damn thing wrong. Every family has rows sometimes. It's not always smooth sailing. In *Dallas* there are rows, desperate situations. (Letter 3)

> Do you know why I like watching it? I think it's because those problems and intrigues, the big and little pleasures and troubles occur in our own lives too. You just don't recognize it and we are not so wealthy as they are. In real life too I know a horror like J.R., but he's just an ordinary builder. That's why I see so many aspects and phases of life, of your own life, in it. Yes, it's really ordinary daily problems more than anything that occur in it and that you recognize. And then it's so marvellous the way they solve them better than you've solved your own problems. (Letter 4)

> You have to see the reality of life, and reality occurs there the

way it is in real life too, the intrigues, especially with people living together in the same house. The wealth is the only difference, I'm not rich (financially, materially speaking). (Letter 6)

I'll tell you why I like watching *Dallas* and what I find so disgusting about it. The good thing about it is that so many different things in it are taken from life, so to speak. Such as Miss Ellie's illness, and Sue Ellen with her marital problems. . . . The disgusting thing I find is the exaggeratedly difficult life these people (in the serial) have, this one's having a great row with that one, and they keep climbing in and out of one another's beds. I get really fed up with that. But that's life, just look around you. There are so few people left living happily and harmoniously with one another. (Letter 10)

I also find some elements true to life. Take the story of Sue Ellen. (Letter 11)

But *Dallas* could really happen. . . . For example, I can sit very happy and fascinated watching someone like Sue Ellen. That woman can really get round us, with her problems and troubles. She is really human. I could be someone like that too. In a manner of speaking. (Letter 2)

Two things stand out in these extracts. The first is that the writers find *Dallas* 'taken from life'; what happens to the Ewing family is in their own eyes not essentially different from what they themselves (can) experience in life. The second point is more important for us, for it reveals the mechanism used for realizing this at first sight puzzling 'experience of reality': in order to be able to experience *Dallas* as 'taken from life' these letter-writers seem to abstract from the denotative level of the text. In naming the 'true to life' elements of *Dallas* the concrete living circumstances in which the characters are depicted (and their wealth in particular springs to mind here) are, it is true, striking but not of significance as regards content; the concrete situations and complications are rather regarded as symbolic representations of more general living experiences: rows, intrigues, problems, happiness and misery. And it is precisely in this sense that these letter-writers find *Dallas* 'realistic'. In other words, at a connotative level they ascribe mainly emotional meanings to *Dallas*. In this sense the realism of *Dallas* can be called an 'emotional realism'.

And now it begins to become clear why the two previous conceptions of realism discussed above, empiricist realism and classical realism, are so unsatisfactory when we want to understand the experience of realism of *Dallas* fans. For however much the two approaches are opposed to one another – for the former realism is a token for a 'good' text, and for the latter for a 'bad' text – in both a cognitive-rationalistic idea dominates: both are based on the assumption that a realistic text offers *knowledge* of the 'objective' social reality. According to the empiricist-realists a text is realistic (and therefore good) if it supplies 'adequate knowledge' of reality, while in the second conception a classic-realistic text is bad because it only creates an illusion of knowledge. But the realism experience of the *Dallas* fans quoted bears no relation to this cognitive level – it is situated at the emotional level: what is recognized as real is not knowledge of the world, but a subjective experience of the world: a 'structure of feeling'.[35]

It is emotions which count in a structure of feeling. Hence emotions form the point of impact for a recognition of a certain type of structure of feeling in *Dallas*; the emotions called up are apparently what remain with the letter-writers most. Thus the following letter-writer describes *Dallas* as a sequence of ever-changing emotions:

Now I'll tell you why I like watching *Dallas*. Here goes!
1. There is suspense in it.
2. It can also be romantic.
3. There is sadness in it.
4. And fear.
5. And happiness.
In short, there is simply everything in that film. (Letter 16)

What we can deduce from this is the notion that in life emotions are always being stirred up, i.e. that life is characterized by an endless fluctuation between happiness and unhappiness, that life is a question of falling down and getting up again. This structure of feeling can be called the *tragic* structure of feeling; tragic because of the idea that happiness can never last for ever but, quite the contrary, is precarious. In the tragic structure of feeling emotional ups and downs occupy a central place: 'All that rowing and lovemaking I find marvellous to watch' (Letter 9). Isn't it precisely the radical contrast between the emotional associations of quarrelling and lovemaking that is so fascinating for her?

Life presents a problem according to the tragic structure of feeling, but that does not mean that life consists solely of problems. On the contrary, problems are only regarded as problems if there is a prospect of their solution, if, in other words, there is hope for better times. Here too we are dealing with a contrast between misery and happiness. So it is not so odd that some letter-writers want to place emphasis on 'happiness':

> Why do I watch *Dallas* every Tuesday? Mainly because of Pamela and that wonderful love between her and Bobby. When I see those two I feel warmth radiating from them. . . . I also find the relationship between Jock and Miss Ellie nice, but I'm scarcely interested at all in J.R. and Sue Ellen and certainly not in the Ewing empire. (Letter 8)

It seems as though the 'wonderful love' of Pamela and Bobby takes on greater glory against the background of the loveless relationship between J.R. and Sue Ellen. According to another letter-writer, lovelessness is even the normal condition: 'Mutual relationships and communications are often so cool that it seems as though they are just wrapped up in themselves' (Letter 7). Or, as expressed briefly but succinctly by one letter-writer: 'a bed of roses it is not' (Letter 6).

Between reality and fiction

Let us summarize what has been said above. Many letter-writers contend that the pleasure of *Dallas* comes from the 'lifelike' character of the serial. If we subject their statements to closer analysis, then it appears that what is experienced as 'real' indicates above all a certain structure of feeling which is aroused by the programme: the tragic structure of feeling. In this many letter-writers who like *Dallas* seem to recognize themselves, and therefore experience it as 'real'. And precisely this recognition arouses pleasure: 'I myself enjoy *Dallas* and the tears start to flow when anything tragic happens (in nearly every episode then)' (Letter 14).

The realism of *Dallas* is therefore produced by the construction of a *psychological* reality, and is not related to its (illusory) fit to an externally perceptible (social) reality. It could even be said that in *Dallas* an 'inner realism' is combined with an 'external unrealism'. The external manifestation of the fictional world of *Dallas* does also contribute to pleasure, not because of its reality value though, but because of its stylization:

a bit of a show, expensive clothes, beautiful horses. (Letter 11)

the serial is very relaxing to watch: beautiful people, a carefree life, restful surroundings. (Letter 19)

I also pay attention to the clothes, make-up and hair-dos. (Letter 1)

Then it's nice to see the clothes of the *Dallas* women. (Letter 9)

There are a few minor details(!) which make the serial attractive, such as the splendid house and the beautiful landscape. (Letter 2)

I started watching *Dallas* just to see the American city scene: the beautiful apartment blocks (especially the really beautiful ones you see during the titles) and the cars. (Letter 21)

It is probably the glamorous *mise-en-scène* of *Dallas* referred to in these letter extracts that is responsible for the fact that viewers are well aware they are watching a fictional world. The illusion of reality is therefore not total. Moreover, the fictional world is not uncritically accepted either. Various letter-writers show quite explicitly that they are aware that *Dallas* is a textual construction.

> You have to keep in mind the reality of life, and there's reality in it too the way it is in real life . . . Although now and then I do find things a bit over the top. (Letter 6)

> The good thing about it, I think, is that lots of things happen in it taken from life, so to speak. Such as . . . Sue Ellen with her marital problems, though I do find that in the longer run that is a bit overdone, she makes a game out of it. I think the serial writers do that deliberately, because lots of men find it terrific to watch her. And would even like to help her. Oh well. Those gallant Don Juans. (Letter 10)

> If they (the writers) write Pamela (or Bobby) out of the serial it will be over for me. The good relationship between those two is my reason for watching. But then, I still believe in 'true love'. (Letter 8)

All these remarks suggest a distance between the 'real' and the fictional world. And precisely because the letter-writers are aware of this, it appears, they can indulge in the excessive emotions aroused in *Dallas*.

> After a serial like that of poverty and misery, where spiritual character is concerned, because financially nothing is lacking, I often think with relief, now I can come back to my own world and I'm very happy in it. To have seen all those worries gives me a nice feeling – you're looking for it, you're bringing it on yourself. (Letter 10)

> Yes, it's actually ordinary daily problems that occur in it mainly and that you recognize. And then it's so marvellous that they solve them better than you've solved your own

problems. Perhaps for me it's relativizing my own problems and troubles or just escaping them. (Letter 4)

'Escape.' This word definitely sounds familiar. It is a term with a negative charge: it is generally not viewed as a sign of strength or courage if people seek refuge in a non-existent fantasy world. It is regarded as a lack of 'sense of reality'. Furthermore, the term often comes up in public discourses over mass entertainment: it is their supposed 'escapist' character that so often leads to a negative judgement of popular entertainment forms.[36] But precisely the fact that this view is so current should warn us to be cautious when we encounter it in the letters. What is the term 'escape' actually referring to, what does it mean for the letter-writers themselves? The term is misleading, because it presupposes a strict division between reality and fantasy, between 'sense of reality' and 'flight from reality'. But is it not rather the case that there is interaction between the two? One of the letter-writers formulates it as follows:

The reason I like watching it is that it's nice to get dizzy on their problems. And you know all along that everything will turn out all right. In fact it's a flight from reality. I myself am a realistic person and I know that reality is different. Sometimes too I really enjoy having a good old cry with them. And why not? In this way my other bottled-up emotions find an outlet. (Letter 5)

'And you know all along that everything will turn out all right.' This is a key sentence, clearly defining the nature of the 'flight'. The 'flight' into a fictional fantasy world is not so much a denial of reality as playing with it. A game that enables one to place the limits of the fictional and the real under discussion, to make them fluid. And in that game an imaginary participation in the fictional world is experienced as pleasurable:

I really like watching it, and especially Pamela and Bobby

because it comes over (in the film) as real affection, although it's only a film. (Letter 6)

I try to find more and more in the various characters. After each shocking event I try to imagine what they'll do. . . . In future there will be more sex in the serial. That is one aspect of a further illustration of the characters. But there are many more. It would be good too if the actors' thoughts were put in. (Letter 7)

I find it's marvellous to project myself into *Dallas* and in my mind to give J.R. a good hiding when he's just pulled off yet another dirty trick, or admire Miss Ellie because she always tries to see the best in everyone or to bring it out in them. Also, I find it awfully nice to imagine myself in that world, such as: 'What would I do if Sue Ellen said that to me?' Or to see myself running round in a big city like Dallas. (Letter 13)

Thus, whatever there is to be said about the pleasure of *Dallas*, the field of tension between the fictional and the real seems to play an important part in it. Or, as a more theoretically minded letter-writer put it: 'It is easier and loads more pleasurable to dash away a tear because Ma Dallas has cancer – because she's only acting – than because of whatever annoying things are in your own life, and at least you have got rid of that tear' (Letter 22). A constant to and fro movement between identification with and distancing from the fictional world as constructed in the text therefore characterizes the involvement of the letter-writers who like *Dallas*. But one question still remains unanswered. How does Dallas succeed in producing those tears, that 'dizziness'? In other words, how does *Dallas* construct the tragic structure of feeling which is recognized by these viewers? This is the subject of the next chapter.

2

DALLAS
and the melodramatic imagination

DALLAS and genre

A television serial like *Dallas* is made according to certain rules
and conventions which belong to a specific genre. A genre is,
one might say, a complex of themes, narrative structures and
styles that groups of individual films or television programmes
have in common with one another.[1] Because we know these
rules and conventions, and have become familiar with them,
we often know quite quickly whether a film is a Western or a
thriller and we entertain certain expectations of the course of
the film, although each Western or thriller has its own idiosyn-
crasies. But the general characteristics of the genre set limits on
the individual genre film, which renders it simpler for the
audience to follow. A genre is in other words a formula and
each individual genre film is a specific 'application' of the rules
and conventions of the genre. This application can succeed to
greater or lesser degree, be more or less inventive, opening new
ground for the genre to a greater or lesser degree. In analysing a
genre film, then, one must constantly move between the general

and the particular, between the established structures and the specific application. In this chapter we shall be trying to do that with *Dallas*.

In order to discover which television genre *Dallas* should be classified under, we must take a look at the structural characteristics of this serial. The first structural characteristic that deserves our attention is its episodic character. For as we shall see later on, this genre-characteristic plays an essential role in the construction of the emotional realism stemming from the tragic structure of feeling.

The episodic character of television fiction can assume two forms: that of the *series*, in which the individual episodes are completely separate from one another from a narrative viewpoint (only the hero(ine) of the series and the basic situation are the connecting elements between the individual episodes), and the *serial*, i.e. the continuous narrative. Programmes like *Magnum* and *Charlie's Angels* are examples of series, while *Dallas*, but also *Hill Street Blues*, are examples of the serial. The separate episodes of a serial cannot in principle be watched in any order, because the precise sequence of the episodes creates a notion of the continuance of time, a continuance which is linear and irreversible. Of course each episode is more or less a separate whole: not only is there in each episode of *Dallas* one more or less central narrative line, but each episode also gets its own title and is divided off by recognizable beginning and end credits.

But in contrast to a series, in which the time between two episodes is of no narrative importance whatever, the time between two episodes in a serial does play a role – though merely an imaginary one – in the way in which viewers experience the narrative. 'The characters in a serial, when abandoned at the end of an episode, pursue an "unrecorded existence" until the next one begins', states Christine Geraghty, in a summary of the formal characteristics of the television serial.[2] The television serial thus appeals to a historical sense of time: it constructs the feeling that the lives of the characters go on during our absence – i.e. between two episodes. Thus the idea of 'unchronicled growth' is aroused in viewers.

This feeling can, however, only arise if the end of an episode offers the possibility for it. The end of an episode of a serial is mostly in the shape of a so-called 'cliffhanger': the narrative is broken off at a moment of very great suspense, so that the viewers are encouraged to see the following episode if they want to know how the story goes on. In earlier film serials the cliffhanger consisted mainly in an abruptly broken off action: or at the very moment the hero threatens to be pushed over the cliff by his enemy, the words 'to be continued' appear – as if to tease the audience – on the screen. The following episode then takes up the thread at the same action, at the same moment in the story. In such cases there is no question of an imaginary passage of time between two episodes.

This type of 'cliffhanger' is, however, seldom used in television serials,[3] although they do occur in fact, by way of exception, in *Dallas*. Just think of the episodes that ended with an attempt on J.R.'s life or with the moment when Southfork is going up in flames. But in by far the majority of cases in *Dallas* a psychological cliffhanger is used: an episode ends most often at the moment when one of the characters lands in a new, psychologically conflictual situation. The last shot of an episode is then nearly always a close-up of the face of the character concerned, which emphasizes the psychological conflict she or he is in. In one of the following episodes – it does not necessarily need to be the very next one – we are then shown how she or he handles the conflict, but meanwhile time proceeds and life goes on as normal. The very next episode usually begins with a new day. Such a construction offers viewers the possibility of having the feeling that time in *Dallas* more or less keeps pace with the time in which the viewers themselves are living. This fact in itself takes care of a specific dimension of 'everyday realism' – the life of the Ewings in Dallas flows on just like our own life.

But an even more important characteristic of *Dallas* that helps to arouse this idea is the fact that there is no narrative ending in sight. The structure of the *Dallas* narrative is radically different from that of a feature film or an episode of a series such as *Kojak* or *Lou Grant*. In classic narrative theory narrative is defined in terms of the schema: order/disturbance of order/restoration of order. A narrative consists of 'a movement between equilibriums which are similar but not identical':[4] at the end all the problems which have disturbed the equilibrium of the opening situation have been resolved. This narrative scheme, however, will not work for an endlessly running television serial like *Dallas*. Although in each episode problems are solved, at the same time new ones are created, which form the point of departure for the following episodes, and so on and so on.

The 'endless' character of a serial is typical for a special genre of television fiction: the soap opera. Soap opera is a long-standing radio genre which was 'invented' and developed at the end of the 1920s by American, mainly female, radio programme makers. The soap opera, which rapidly developed into one of the most popular entertainment forms on radio, was characterized by an accent on human relations, domesticity and daily life; it is home, garden and kitchen problems which are discussed and solved by the characters.[5] The 'soaps', so called because it was mainly soap manufacturers who sponsored the programmes, shot up like mushrooms and built up a faithful following, especially among housewives – not least because they were broadcast almost every day. The soap opera was alleged to be able to provide some (surrogate) company for housewives living in isolation; they listened to their favourite soaps while doing the ironing, cooking or other domestic work.[6]

With the coming of television the soap opera finally disappeared from the American radio stations, but the genre took on a new and flourishing existence in the new medium. Although soap opera is not an exclusively American phenomenon — British, Australian and Brazilian television, for example, are richly provided with home-grown soap operas — the genre is almost totally unknown on Dutch television. *Peyton Place* and *Coronation Street* could be seen at the beginning of the 1970s on Dutch television, and they were quite popular, but the American 'daytime serials', as they are officially called, have never been screened in the Netherlands — in contrast to the parodies of them: *Mary Hartman! Mary Hartman!* and *Soap!* which are esteemed mainly by an intellectual audience! Only with the arrival of *Dallas* on the screen did the Dutch television audience get handed another American soap opera.

But *Dallas* is not a daytime soap opera. Just like *Peyton Place*, *Dallas* is made to be shown at prime time. Of course this has its consequences. An important formal difference between *Dallas* and the daytime soap opera is the much greater attention to visualization in *Dallas*. In contrast to daytime soaps, which have always kept a radio-like character and in which the visual element is kept to a minimum (very sparse locations, very simple camera work, etc.), *Dallas* looks chic — because of the high production values which generally apply for prime time programmes — and it is made with filmic expertise. A lot of attention is paid to the visual attractiveness of the locations, the stars' costumes, and so on. This is doubtless a background which should not be neglected when accounting for its world-wide popularity. The hegemony of American television (and film) has habituated the world public to American production values and American *mises-en-scène*, such as the vast prairie or the big cities, the huge houses with expensive interiors, luxurious and fast cars and, last but not least, the healthy- and good-looking men and women, white, not too young, not too old. Such images have become signs which no longer merely indicate something like 'Americanness', but visual pleasure as such. The television audience has, over the years, become familiar with all this and tends to recognize it as pleasurable; it is as though for large groups of people these American images fulfil a signal function, they imply the promise that the story will be suspenseful and exciting. As Simon Frith states: 'America, as experienced in films and music, has itself become the object of consumption, a symbol of pleasure.'[7]

The fact that *Dallas* is a prime time programme also has consequences for the structure of the narrative content. Prime time is the time in which the whole family usually watches television, in contrast to the morning or afternoon hours (during which housewives, pensioners and the unemployed form the largest group of viewers). A popular programme must therefore, at least according to the commercial logic of the American television industry, appeal to the whole family. In a certain sense this could explain why in *Dallas* themes from other genres such as the Western are worked in, to attract the interest of a broad mass audience. Similarly the fact that men and masculine themes such as business life play a much more central part in *Dallas* than in the average daytime soap could be connected to this.[8] Therefore *Dallas* is not a soap opera in the traditional sense.

DALLAS as prime time soap opera

But in spite of the differences we have cited between *Dallas* and the daytime soaps, there are sufficient structural similarities between them to justify calling *Dallas*, as an American television encyclopedia[9] has done, a 'prime time soap opera'. The similarities lie in the first place in the narrative structure dictated by the endless character of the serial. Each episode of a soap opera always consists of various narratives running parallel. In every episode one of these narratives gets the greatest emphasis, but the other narratives keep 'simmering' as it were in the background, to reach a climax in some subsequent episode. As one letter-writer puts it:

> I watch *Dallas* pretty regularly because I find it a free serial. By that I mean that the writer can go in any direction in every

episode. One time Bobby is the central figure, then it can be J.R. or Sue Ellen or another member of that 'immense' family. (Letter 5)

In this sense a soap opera is therefore a continuous coming and going of mini-narratives, in an uneven rhythm. This characteristic of the soap opera can explain why many letter-writers who dislike *Dallas* find it longwinded: 'Every time I watch it again I'm curious as to what has happened. But then *Dallas* ends and even more questions have arisen. I find that really stupid' (Letter 37). But this 'longwindedness', this steady continuance of the story, this 'indefinitely expandable middle',[10] is essential for the soap opera as genre. Those who like *Dallas* will therefore tacitly agree to this convention. They are not expecting the definitive dénouement; quite the contrary, the (promise of) endlessness itself is a source of pleasure. 'I can't get enough of it' (Letter 9), says one letter-writer. According to Sheila Johnston, the primary source of involvement in a soap opera is not situated in the *suspense* of the narrative, as in many other popular television genres, but in 'the creation and slow consolidation of a complex fictional world'.[11] The repetitive character of *Dallas* can therefore be very important for *Dallas* fans:

It's reassuring to see the same characters again and again. Then you are far more involved in it. At least, I feel that. When I sit down to watch, I always get the idea that I belong to the family in a way too, because I have seen so much of them. I can enter into all the characters, because they are so familiar. I know them through and through. (Letter 20)

But there are other characteristics which are typical for the structure of the soap opera and which also apply for *Dallas*. Not only do different narratives exist side by side, sometimes to touch and intersect one another, and sometimes to run completely parallel. The fact that not just one (or a few) but many main characters are involved is also an important aspect of soap operas. Of none of the main characters in *Dallas* can it be said that he or she occupies the most important position from a narrative viewpoint. (In the press, it is often assumed that J.R. is the main character in *Dallas*. Although his actions do in fact often play a central part in the propulsion of the narrative, to reduce all the other characters to secondary roles shows a misjudgement of the multi-dimensionality of the *Dallas* narrative. Furthermore, considering J.R. as the main character only results from a very specific reading, which may be characterized by a masculine bias. For many letter-writers the role of J.R. is not that important at all; they are not that interested in him.)

In fact the unity of the soap opera is not created by all the individual characters together, but by the community in which they live. In that community (Dallas) they each occupy an established position. This community also appears to determine which possibilities of action are open to the various characters. Not a single one of the characters escapes the 'rules' of that community; in this sense the soap-community is an enclosed community, like a village, a street, a hospital. Although new characters can enter the community – and that happens regularly: the soap opera steadily encroaches as it were on its surroundings in the course of years – as soon as they have made their entrance they are subjected to the laws and the logic of the community.

In *Dallas* the Ewing family forms the centre of the community. At the beginning of the serial Jock, Miss Ellie, J.R., Sue Ellen, Bobby, Pamela and Lucy have an established structural position within the family, positions ('father', 'mother', 'son', 'daughter-in-law', 'husband', 'wife', 'granddaughter') which are pretty unalterable. Of course later on alterations do occur in the status of the characters within the family: for example, Sue Ellen first divorces J.R. and later marries him again; and Ray Krebbs was initially not a member of the family then later turns out to be an (illegitimate) son of Jock's, so that suddenly he does belong to the family. But the fact remains that within the family itself the positions are established. The family is the central point of reference. Gillian Swanson, who has analysed the narrative structure of *Dallas*, has shown that 'it is their identity as a family which is the central standard around which relations are made and according to which characters are defined and events are constructed'.[12]

The Ewing family is a community within the wider community of *Dallas*, for other characters who do not belong to the family belong to that larger community. Of these characters Cliff Barnes is certainly the most important: he is the personification of the counter-forces within the larger community which try to disrupt the Ewing family. The community as a whole is therefore by no means a harmonious one – on the contrary, conflict and strife are the order of the day.

This brings us to a third important characteristic of the soap opera. This concerns the themes of the story. A soap opera follows the individual lives of the characters of a community, but it is not interested in their whole lives. In other words, it does not reveal all their doings, all their experiences. The soap opera is selective; it tells us a lot about the different characters, but it also leaves large parts of their life histories untold. A familiar complaint levelled at soap operas is, for example, that they lack social relevance: social problems and conflicts get short shrift or are not dealt with in an adequate, that is, structural way. But anyone expressing such a criticism overlooks the fact that leaving out or cutting out questions which are seen as important in the social reality is functional for the soap opera as genre. In other words, the soap opera generally ignores too concrete social or cultural references because it concerns itself with a completely different aspect of life.

According to Charlotte Brunsdon the ideological problematic of soap opera, that is, the perspective from which events in the narrative take on meaning, is that of 'personal life'. 'More particularly, personal life in its everyday realization through personal relationships. This can be understood to be constituted primarily through the representation of romances, families, and the attendant rituals – births, engagements, marriages, divorces and deaths.'[13] However, this does not imply that only the so-called private sphere of life is dealt with. Questions from the public sphere have a place too. The way in which they are handled and take on meaning is, however, always from the standpoint of the private sphere: 'the action of soap opera is not restricted to the familial, or quasi-familial institutions, but as it were *colonizes* the public masculine sphere, representing it from the point of view of the personal', writes Brunsdon.[14] Thus in *Dallas* the business imbroglios to do with Ewing Oil are always shown with an eye to their consequences for the mutual relations of the family members. And the motives of Cliff Barnes in his work – first as politician and lawyer, later as owner and manager of a rival concern – are as it were shrivelled down to that one, all-prevailing motive: revenge on the Ewings. In short, in the world of the soap opera all sorts of events and situations from the public sphere occur only in so far as they lead to problems and complications in the private sphere.

The striking thing is, however, that these problems and complications assume such grotesque shapes. Personal life in soap operas is dominated by conflicts and catastrophes, which are blown up to improbable proportions. None of the following sensational problems has not yet occurred in *Dallas*: murder, suspicion of murder, marital crisis, adultery, alcoholism, rare disease, miscarriage, rape, airplane accident, car accident, kidnapping, corruption, psychiatric treatment, and so on. It is precisely this characteristic of the soap opera, this endless piling up of appalling crises, which often gives rise to incomprehension and ridicule from critics. For example, one well-known Dutch doctor and writer has lamented of *Dallas*: 'I find it admirable the things these people can put up with, for . . . after a tenth of that stress I would be lying in the psychiatric hospital.'[15]

As a prime time soap, then, *Dallas* combines the ideological problematic and the narrative structure of the daytime soaps with the visual style and glamour which are more usual for prime time programmes.

DALLAS as melodrama

Until now we have been describing the most important formal characteristics of *Dallas* as soap opera. Now I want to illustrate how important this formal structure is for the construction of the tragic structure of feeling – the complex of meanings which, as indicated in the last chapter, viewers can read from *Dallas*. Note: *can* read. The tragic structure of feeling as an umbrella meaning of *Dallas* emerges from the level of connotation, and not all viewers will ascribe the same connotative meanings to the programme. In other words, an arousal of the tragic structure of feeling is certainly made possible by the way in which the soap opera text itself is formally and ideologically structured, but whether this meaning is also actually ascribed depends on the cultural orientations of the viewers concerned: the expectations they have of the serial, their attitude towards the genre and television in general, the place television viewing occupies in their life, and so on. In the following chapter we shall see that *Dallas* can also give rise to quite different reactions; that the tragic structure of feeling suggested in it can also provoke ridicule and irony. Moreover, the individual viewer will probably not always make the same emotional associations when watching the programme; it is more plausible to assume that he or she can be gripped at one moment by the tragic structure of feeling, and at another moment can assume a more ironic attitude towards the text – identification and distancing constantly alternate with one another. The tragic structure of feeling is not therefore contained as it were in the nature of *Dallas*. It is a complex of meanings which is central for certain groups of *Dallas* fans, for whom a tragic look into daily life is in principle logical and meaningful.

There is a name for cultural genres whose main effect is the stirring up of the emotions: melodrama. Melodrama is a drama form which is not highly regarded in our culture and is mostly dismissed as 'a sentimental, artificially plotted drama that sacrifices characterization to extravagant incident, makes sensational appeals to the emotions of its audience, and ends on a happy or at least a morally assuring note.'[16] Not all soap operas or aspects of a soap opera can be regarded as melodramatic. The English soap opera *Coronation Street*, for example, has a more socio-realistic nature.[17] Most American soap operas, however, certainly are very melodramatic in character. So is *Dallas*, as I shall illustrate below.

It is difficult to persuade people to take melodrama seriously as a cultural form which is a significant expression of a lived reality, because, according to current notions, it plays on the emotions of the public in a false way: emotional straining after effect is seen as its sole aim. It is also sometimes said that melodrama is failed tragedy: the plot is so exaggerated and overdone that the story becomes ridiculous and bereft of any credibility and sensibility. The characters in a melodrama seem to be so taken up with their own violent emotions that there is no scope for reflection, intellectual distancing and relativizing.

What is unsatisfactory with these attitudes is not so much their descriptive value as the fusion of description and judgement. Melodrama is a cultural form that has been popular since the beginning of the nineteenth century, especially among the 'popular' classes, and as such has also always had the status of inferior culture. And indeed, in the eyes of the literary and literate European culture of the established bourgeoisie, capitalizing on plot at the expense of giving greater depth to the characters is a reason for rejecting melodrama as 'cliché-ridden' and 'banal'. But such a judgement is one-sided, not only because it makes absolute the norms of the European literary tradition, but also because it looks only at the surface, the outward form of melodrama. For us this last point is of particular interest. The application of literary norms to melodrama disregards the *function* of the heightened plot and the exaggerated emotions, while it is this very function that can reveal something of the attraction of melodrama. For what comes over from outside as a simplistic and easy-going penchant for the sensational, can in its structure constitute the strength of the genre.

In *Dallas* too we can perceive this penchant for the sensational: the crises in the Ewings' family life succeed one another at an incredibly rapid speed, at least compared with 'real' life. But although such a plot structure will be viewed by outsiders as pure sensationalism, within the fictional world of *Dallas* it is not sensational at all. On the contrary, such a plot structure is quite normal for the soap opera. To put it more strongly, soap opera would not be able to exist without murders, legal battles, extramarital affairs or serious illness. So it seems that the genre acquires its very strength from such exaggerated occurrences. This at least is the view advanced by the American television critic Horace Newcomb. 'The fact that this story, in the technical reality of soap opera, is so unsensational gives us the clue to its real importance', he states.[18] In the world of soap opera the characters go through all kinds of calamities as though it were the most normal thing in life. The significance of such a plot structure is that through it 'human misery' is exposed in a very emphatic manner. 'Most of the problems forming the centre of soap opera plots can be defined best as being in the areas of psychical or emotional pain', says Newcomb,[19] and it seems as though it is not possible to express that pain other than by means of an overdramatizing of the narrative.

Is this the result of a lack of creativity and subtlety? I do not believe that such a personal reproach levelled at the writers of melodramatic soap operas gives us any insight into the cultural specificity of the genre, as it ignores the structural function of exaggerated plots in soap opera. Exaggerated plots can be regarded as the symbolic lumping together of the diffuse and hard-to-describe notion of 'life's torments' which occur at times in every individual life. They function as metaphors for these 'life's torments'. And the fact that in soap operas the same types of plots are reverted to, the same sorts of narrative situations occur, should not be blamed on a lack of originality, for at this level a soap opera certainly does not try to be original. (Originality on the basis of individual creativity is a bourgeois literary value which cannot be applied to a popular genre such as soap opera.) Rather I would suggest that such plots and situations are dominant and generally current as metaphors for 'life's torments' in our culture, speaking directly to the imagination of the public.

Within the framework of a popular fiction form like soap opera, exaggerated events such as kidnappings, marital dramas and chance meetings with great consequences should not be regarded and assessed for their referential value, but as bearers of the melodramatic effect. Melodrama does not seek to dramatize the unique experience of a single human character (as is mostly the case in 'serious' drama). In a fascinating article on American film melodrama of the 1950s Thomas Elsaesser points out that melodrama operates on a 'non-psychological conception of the *dramatis personae*, who figure less as autonomous individuals than to transmit the action and link the various locales within a total constellation. In this respect, melodramas have a myth-making function, in so far as their significance lies in the structure and articulation of the action, not in any psychologically motivated correspondence with individualized experience.'[20] In other words, the 'psychological credibility' of the characters in melodrama is subordinated to the functioning of those characters in melodramatic situations, so that the emotional effect is pushed to extremes. That effect can be achieved because these imagined situations are socially and culturally surrounded by myths and fantasies which endow them with a strongly emotional appeal. That appeal draws less on the bare facts of those situations than on the metaphorical role they play in the popular imagination.

Alcoholism is one such metaphor which is often used in melodrama to represent the impotence of a character. As Elsaesser remarks:

Although alcoholism is too common an emblem in films [. . .] to deserve a close thematic analysis, drink does become interesting in movies where its dynamic significance is developed and its qualities as a visual metaphor recognized: wherever characters are seen swallowing and gulping their drinks as if they were swallowing their humiliations along with their pride, vitality and the life-force have become palpably destructive and a phoney libido has turned into real anxiety.[21]

The symbolic effectiveness of drunkenness is employed not only in films like John Huston's *Under the Volcano*. Anyone who has followed *Dallas* faithfully will know how Sue Ellen took to drink and regularly appeared drunk on the screen. Her alcoholic inclination was used as a visual externalizing of her feelings of impotence in a life-situation in which she felt fettered: to be married to a man whom she loathed and who was unfaithful to her, but who at the same time had her completely in his power. Sue Ellen's alcoholism therefore has a metaphorical function here: the intention is not so much that viewers start worrying about the concrete drinking problem (from a financial point of view, for example, it will never be any problem for Sue Ellen to get a drink: pots of money), much rather, the depiction of alcoholism should enable viewers to have some idea of Sue Ellen's psychological state, of her suffering, of the emotional conflicts she is battling with.

Such a metaphor derives its strength from a *lack* of originality and uniqueness: precisely because it constantly recurs in all sorts of popular narratives, it takes on for viewers a direct comprehensibility and recognizability. We could even say that viewers must be ready to read all sorts of events and situations in the narrative in a metaphorical way, in order to be able to understand and evaluate their full implications. Insight into the metaphorical value of the plot is the basis for the pleasure of many faithful viewers of soap operas – an insight missed by the intellectual who only watches a soap opera now and then with a mistrustful attitude and seeks to evaluate the narrative only on the basis of its literary value.

I cannot go into the question here of why exactly these events and situations fulfil a metaphorical function and precisely which common-sense meanings they contain. That would require a separate cultural-historical essay. Why, for example, in addition to murders, misfortunes or diseases are there so many illegitimate children, unknown fathers or mothers (for whom the adult children passionately and restlessly search), or secret pasts (with fatal results for the present)? All these plot elements are incorporated in *Dallas* too! In *Dallas*, however, not only are existing metaphors adapted in the narrative in an ingenious way, but these metaphors are sometimes modernized as well, adapted to the sensibilities of the present.

An example is the metaphor of illness. It is not surprising that characters in melodramas and soap operas are so often ill, as this can propel the narrative forward in a marvellously melo-dramatic way. As Susan Sontag has illustrated, the phenom-enon of illness is liberally surrounded by all sorts of emotional-ly loaded associations and images. Being ill means not only physically being out of order but also being excluded from the world of the healthy, being overcome by an unknown and uncontrollable force, etc. And some illnesses, such as tubercu-losis and cancer, have a uniquely terrifying aura. Being ill therefore has far-reaching cultural consequences extending far beyond the biological fact of illness itself.[22]

In soap operas there are often cases of illness for which the diagnosis remains unknown or the physical results of which remain invisible. For example, in *Dallas* Cliff Barnes and Pamela Ewing at a certain moment are told the unpleasant news by their doctor that they are suffering from an incurable illness inherited from their father Digger, called 'neurofibro-matosis' – a mysterious illness which does exist according to the medical encyclopedia, but the symptoms of which in fact are not such as they are shown in *Dallas*! But only a killjoy would point that out. It is not the illness itself that is relevant for the narrative, but the dramatic consequences of it for the sick person. In the case of Pamela the illness functions as a metaphor for the drama that a powerful desire can never be fulfilled: beyond her own control, she can never achieve what she wants (to have children), for the illness prevents her. (Later the plot becomes even more involved when it emerges that Pamela is not Digger's daughter at all. . . .)

In stark contrast to the vagueness of Pamela's illness, however, is the hard realism of the illness that strikes Miss Ellie: breast cancer. From a content-analysis it has emerged that the diagnosis of cancer hardly ever occurs in soap operas:[23] the illness is apparently so terrifyingly real that it cannot be fitted into the mythical world of soap opera. The fact that it does occur in *Dallas* and in such an emphatic way (two episodes were totally taken up by Miss Ellie's illness), can be regarded as 'modern' or in any case as daring, the more so as Miss Ellie's breast cancer is dramatically mobilized as a metaphor for a form of 'life's torment' which certainly does not enjoy any general social recognition: the sexual objectifying of the female body by men. Miss Ellie realizes that a mastectomy has far-reaching results for her attractiveness to men. She does not believe what her husband Jock says: that it makes no difference to him (for, she muses, 'he has an eye for a pretty girl') and she tells him that men cannot understand what she is feeling. From other scenes it emerges how Miss Ellie's mastectomy releases a feeling of menace among the other female family members (Sue Ellen, Pamela and Lucy) which has to do with their sexual identity. In particular for Lucy the thought of such a mutilation of the body is so unbearable that at first she refuses to see the sick Miss Ellie and has to be persuaded by Pamela to visit her grandmother in the hospital. For Miss Ellie herself too, the illness leaves deep traces for years. Although initially she seems to recover well from the illness and has been able apparently to forget the torment, years later her mutilated body causes her to shrink from entering a new marriage – with Clayton Farlow – a fear which she has to be argued out of by Donna Krebbs ('He loves you!'). In this way a theme which has been brought into the open by feminists is recycled in *Dallas*!

As melodramatic soap opera therefore, *Dallas*, by means of 'a sentimental, artificially plotted drama that sacrifices characterization to extravagant incident' makes visible areas of internal psychological disturbance. It is now time to go into the nature of these disturbances in a little more detail.

DALLAS and family tragedy

'What is implausible in [television melodramas] is the continual necessity for emotional display by the characters. In real life we are rarely called upon to feel so intensely, and never in such neatly escalating sequences. But the emotions dramatized by these improbable plots are not in themselves unreal, or at least they need not be', states David Thornburn in an article on television melodrama.[24] It is just as though, under the guise of the sensational, something is brought to the surface which otherwise would remain hidden. The sensational improbability of the narrative must magnify the probability of the conflicts expressed by it.

In most soap operas the conflicts forming the foundation of the dramatic development of the narrative always have to do with difficult family situations: it is the conflictual relations between family members – husband/wife, parents/children, brothers/sisters – which again and again give rise to tensions, crises and emotional outbursts. We have indicated earlier that the ideological problematic of the soap opera is personal life; we can now add that, certainly in *Dallas*, the development of personal life *within the family* is set up as the ideological norm. The family is regarded as the ideal cradle for human happiness. At least, it should be.

This focusing on the area of the personal and on the problem of psychological well-being distinguishes the soap opera in a crucial way from other genres of popular television fiction, such as the police or adventure series. These genres are pre-occupied with overcoming a danger or an enemy, and there is usually little room there for emotional uncertainties or psychological conflicts relating to individual, personal existence. The (almost always male) hero is in this regard completely sure of himself. Even more, precisely this certainty forms an important ingredient of his invincibility: he never doubts, knows precisely what he has to do and never dwells on his own insignificance. He is invulnerable.

This type of popular fiction appeals to the public in a radically different way from soap opera. Just as in film melodrama, 'its excitement comes from conflict not between enemies but between people tied by blood or love'.[25] That is why there is no invincibility in soap operas: as a value, invincibility does not count in family relationships. Even J.R., who shrinks from nothing and no one to get his way, from time to time has to face the fact that he can lose. And that applies even more for all the other characters. No one is invulnerable, however heroic, powerful or strong he or she might be. Which is tragic.

Family life is not actually romanticized in soap operas; on the contrary, the imaginary ideal of the family as safe haven in a heartless world is constantly shattered. In *Dallas* this is done in an extremely sophisticated way. In contrast to most traditional soap operas *Dallas* concentrates totally on the ups and downs of one family: the Ewings. All the actions in the narrative are ultimately directed at the position of this family within the *Dallas* community. And for the characters it is of particularly great significance whether they are inside or outside the family. Any new marriage, such as that between Miss Ellie and Clayton Farlow, any divorce, such as between Pamela and Bobby, or the birth of a child also inevitably causes some disturbance, because here the profile of the family is at stake. The continuance of and harmony within the Ewing family is paramount in *Dallas*. Whereas the characters of other soap operas can still find inner peace and happiness outside their family life (such as in the intimacy and camaraderie between two women friends), the belief that one can feel at home in a community not based on family relationships is doomed to failure. Sue Ellen's greatest defeat is that, after she has finally divorced J.R. and tried to build up an independent existence, she nevertheless remarries J.R. and thus – against her better judgement – projects her personal happiness again within the Ewing family. Pamela's happiness too after her divorce from Bobby is only temporary and therefore illusory: Mark, the new man in her life (who is by the way merely a compensation for Bobby, whom she still loves), turns out to be incurably ill and soon dies.

The outside world, i.e. the world outside the family, is presented in *Dallas* as a hotbed of activity threatening to the family. The relationships the Ewing women enter into with people (men) outside the family are, from the standpoint of the family, a danger to the unity of the family. The business contacts of the Ewing men in the Dallas community lead only too often to instability in the family harmony, especially through the continuing discord between J.R. and Bobby. Because the idea of personal happiness can only exist against the background of the unity of the family, this unity must always be safeguarded against attacks from outside and from inside. In short, the conflict between family-strengthening and family-undermining forces is, as Swanson's structural analysis of the *Dallas* narrative shows, the most important motor that propels this soap opera forward.[26]

Family harmony is also offered to the viewers as the norm for the assessment of the situation of the Ewings. The way in which the narrative is told scarcely allows for another point of view. The central role that Southfork plays in each episode, as the place – the haven – where family members sooner or later always return, ensures that the ranch functions as a permanent identification point. The scenes in which the whole family is at home together, at breakfast or in the living room before going to dinner, often form temporary respites in the endless series of complications. One or two of such scenes are included in each episode.[27] This was particularly true of the earlier episodes. The slow disintegration of the original family makes these family gatherings less and less frequent. In one episode there is even a dramatic scene in which Miss Ellie, the *mater familias*, is sitting quite alone at the head of a luxuriously laid dinner table – her children have not turned up, and her husband Jock is dead. . . . The viewers are thus invited to identify with the idea that the unity of the family is a living condition of prime importance. (Such an identification, however, by no means need coincide with a real attachment of the viewer to the ideology of the family: it is a component of the fantasmatic game the viewer begins when he or she enters into the narrative.)

But this norm of family harmony takes its toll. The individual family members are subjected to its demands. It is the family structure which determines which rules each of the family members must conform to; it is from the standpoint of the family that each family member is, as it were, set in a stereotyped role, such as the loving mother or the worthy son. According to Swanson this subjection of the Ewing characters to a stereotyped role forms a second important structural source of conflict.[28] They do not seem capable of becoming reconciled to the shackles of the family ideal, or they actively try to escape from them, and this leads to new, manifest problems. For example, Sue Ellen's attempts to get away from J.R. cannot be reconciled with holding the family intact: she has to leave the family in order to fulfil her own desires (and staying in the family or returning to it means giving up her desires!). Also, her initial refusal to look after her own newborn child – a refusal of the traditional mother role – does not exactly have a favourable effect on the family peace: it leads to worry for Miss Ellie, to reproach from J.R. and to the (brief) illusion for Pamela that she can take over motherhood from Sue Ellen with baby John Ross. Peace only returns when Sue Ellen accepts her duty as a mother. And above all the poisonous activities of J.R., his countless extramarital relations and his business intrigues with Ewing Oil, can certainly not be reconciled with the safeguarding of family harmony. But J.R. is pre-eminently someone who is always consciously abandoning his role of son, brother and husband whenever it suits him, and so puts the unity of the family chronically at risk.

Thus the most important characters move constantly between the two poles of a dilemma: either to go their own way in search of personal happiness, or to submit to the social fetters of the family structure. The moments when these two options are in harmony with one another are few. Just as in any soap opera, no marriage in *Dallas* is proof against the ravages of time, not even the almost idyllic marriage of Pamela and Bobby.

What is conveyed in this representation then is the eternal contradiction, the insolubility of inner conflicts, the unbridgeability as it were of the antithesis between pleasure principle and reality principle. As Laura Mulvey puts it, 'beyond or beneath the dramatic mainspring of ideological contradiction that melodrama plays on, lies another contradiction: the impossibility of reconciling desire with reality. The melodrama recognizes this gap by raising problems, known and recognizable, and offering a personal escape similar to that of a daydream: a chance to work through inescapable frustrations by positing an alternative ideal never seen as more than a momentary illusion.'[29] It is this disturbing 'truth' over personal life that viewers are confronted with. What could provide better soil for the tragic structure of feeling?

Soap opera, melodrama and the tragic structure of feeling

But this tragic structure of feeling within *Dallas* would impose itself in a less forceful way on devoted viewers if the conflicts the characters have to go through were not presented in a specifically melodramatic way. 'Characters caught in the world of melodrama are not allowed transcendent awareness or knowledge', says Mulvey.[30] In other words, although the problems of characters develop from a conflict set structurally in the narrative, the characters themselves are not aware of that structure. They fight for a happier life in the direct immediacy of existence and are not capable of sizing up their objective position. 'The melodramatic characters act out contradiction, achieving actual confrontation to varying degrees and gradually facing impossible resolutions and probable defeats', according to Mulvey.[31] And precisely this *gradual* facing of one's own impotence makes it the more tragic: illusions and ideals are steadily undermined.

The dialogues in *Dallas* – dialogue is *the* narrative instrument of soap opera – never contain any critical and conscious (self) reflection. The characters never ponder on their position in the world, they never philosophize from a detached point of view on themselves and their relations to others. The conversations the characters have with one another, on the other hand, always express the living through or digesting of a conflict, in the here and now. There is never question of an intellectual exposition and exchange of ideas; each spoken word reflects the subjective inner world of a character – his or her desires, fears, moral preferences, etc. But at the same time the dialogues between the characters are not often examples of frank and honest communication. Often they don't say everything, or don't say what they mean, or mean more than they say. In this sense the dialogues in *Dallas* are often elliptical. The status of the spoken word is therefore relativized, as though there are always things which cannot or may not be said. The essence of a situation is not expressed, but lies as it were concealed behind the facial expression of the character who at the end of a scene – as so often in *Dallas* – is shown in close-up and held for a few seconds, before the first shot of the following scene.[32] This melodramatic method produces an enlargement of the tragic structure of feeling: the close-ups emphasize the fact that the character ultimately does not have control of her or his own life, not so much because of the machinations of some superhuman divinity, but because of contradictions inherent in human society itself.

The end of the narrative is always a problem for melodrama. It is often pointed out that a melodrama is only effective when it has an 'open' end: at first sight there may be the possibility of a happy ending, but so many future conflicts are already brewing that the happy end itself is not credible. In fact the end of a melodrama is not actually so important; the main thing is what happens before. As Mulvey notes, 'the strength of the melodramatic form lies in the amount of dust the story raises along the road, a cloud of over-determined irreconcilables which put up a resistance to being neatly settled in the last five minutes.'[33]

However, for the soap opera this problem of the last five minutes is much less acute. It is inherent in the form of soap opera that in principle it goes on endlessly.[34] The soap opera can, therefore, because it is always going along the road, raise an infinite amount of dust without worrying about clearing it up. This lack of an end, this constant deferment of the ultimate 'solution', adds a new dimension to the tragic structure of feeling. The endless repetition of the slogan at the end of each episode of *Soap*!, that tragicomic parody of soap opera, is a striking illustration of this: 'Confused? You won't be after the next episode of . . . *Soap*!' But one is nevertheless confused yet again.

Tania Modleski has pointed out in this connection that in soap opera the so-called 'hermeneutic code' prevails.[35] This code consists of all those elements in a narrative which pose a problem or effect a delay in the solution of a problem: obstacles, errors, devious behaviour, deceptions, half-truths, and so on. In a classic, linear narrative the hermeneutic code is ultimately conquered by the final solution, the moment of complete truth. But in a soap opera delay is the rule, the normal course of affairs. And so the viewer is manoeuvred into a position of permanent expectation which, in the words of Roland Barthes, refers to 'disorder: disorder is [. . .] what is forever added on without solving anything, without finishing anything'.[36] This position of eternal expectation strengthens a feeling of aimlessness and directionlessness; it 'creates a feeling that things are constantly happening (becoming more complicated) in the narrative, but that, at the same time, nothing ever really happens'.[37] The idea of progress, which is connected with the idea of a fundamental difference between past and present, is absent. The characters in *Dallas* live in the prison of an eternally conflictual present. This places the viewer in a curious position. She knows that the soap opera will never end and that the agony will never let up. Whereas in other narratives the assurance and confirmation of a happy end is a source of pleasure, in soap opera it is precisely the tragic knowledge of the *holding off* of an end satisfactory to all the characters which is the basis for narrative pleasure.

Furthermore, the viewer's position towards the individual characters is also ambiguous. As we have said, in a soap opera various narratives always intersect one another. Whereas at one moment we can sympathize with Sue Ellen's marital woes and get a glimpse of her having a good cry at her psychiatrist's, the next moment we are witness to Pamela's dilemma about whether to tell Bobby of her illness. All the characters live their own lives without necessarily having anything to do with or being in touch with the problems, actions and plans of the others. They are wrapped up in their own preoccupations and view any situation purely and simply from their own subjective standpoint. Viewers, however, know 'everything' about each of them and thus find themselves in a powerful, omniscient position. But strangely enough this power is based on a realization of powerlessness, because they know that the relational structure in which the life of all the characters is embedded is immovable and leads to all kinds of tensions, without the characters themselves being aware of them.

An example: Miss Ellie hesitates to tell Jock that she has breast cancer, because she is afraid that then he will turn away from her. (She experiences exactly the same fear, as we have

noted, much later when Clayton has asked her to marry him.)
At the same time Jock does not know how he can tell Miss Ellie
that he was married before, because he is frightened of her
reaction. In both there is doubt and uncertainty, and therefore
mistrust, without their knowing it of one another, which leads
repeatedly to all kinds of irritations and misunderstandings.
Viewers, however, are informed of both secrets and must, in
order to be able to continue to follow the narrative, put
themselves in the position of both. This appeal to 'multiple
identification'[38] means that viewers cannot simply identify
with one character in order to understand and judge all the
developments from that character's point of view, as is mostly
the case in an adventure story.

This floating viewer-position is strengthened even more by
the fact that the characters are sometimes particularly incon-
sistent in their behaviour and within a short period can completely change their attitude. An American television critic has
noted that a total instability of behavioural codes prevails in
Dallas,[39] so that neither the characters themselves nor the
viewers know where they stand. For example, instead of
handing her over to the police, J.R. puts Sue Ellen's sister
Kristin on the plane out of Dallas with a thick wad of bank-
notes, after he has learned that she was the one who had tried to
shoot him. And so Sue Ellen's feelings for J.R. after the attempt
on his life veer right round: although she hated him before, she
suddenly realizes that she does in fact love him . . . only to find
out some weeks later that J.R. does not deserve her love. There
is a lack of 'any secure sense of what constitutes the status quo',
says Sheila Johnston.[40] And Modleski comes to the conclusion
that soap operas implicitly announce a frightful truth about
life: 'soaps continually insist on the insignificance of the individual life'.[41] The world of the soap opera is therefore totally
ambiguous. It is a world in which the area of the personal is
all-prevailing, but in which at the same time all personal lives
are perverted. For not a single individual in a soap opera is free
to construct his or her own life history. On the contrary, it is the

structures and contradictions in which they are caught that determine developments.

In *Dallas*, however, one figure escapes these shackles: J.R. This villain constantly ignores the laws and rules of society and bends developments to his own will. Through his dishonest dealings and intrigues he is the most important cause of misery in *Dallas*. Modleski points out that the villain has an essential function in the soap opera narrative: he or she is the one who does not submit but resists. But paradoxically enough, J.R.'s actions tend to strengthen the tragic structure of feeling. He demonstrates that power can only be coupled with badness and immorality, while those who want to live a 'good' life are constantly bereft of power and doomed to suffer. But that does not mean that the villain always wins. On the contrary, because in the soap opera ambivalence and temporality are the rule, J.R. has to keep on trying to get his way. According to some it is precisely this unremitting and indefatigable attempt to break out which explains the attraction of the villain. As Horace Newcomb says, 'what we see in J.R. is a refusal to give up. He persists.'[42]

But the villain fulfils a second function in the world of soap opera. Not only is he not an outsider, set apart from an otherwise harmonious community, but he also belongs to the community. Moreover, he is the one who brings the community to life and sees to it that things happen. The evil is therefore woven into the order of the community itself, so that the community by definition is conflictual because it bears the core of the conflict within itself: harmony only exists as unattainable Utopia. Thus, the Ewing family and *Dallas* would certainly cease to exist if J.R. were put out of action: family life, in the logic of *Dallas*, can only exist by the grace of the one who regularly jeopardizes the very survival of the family!

Finally, let us return to the meaning of the glamorous *mise-en-scène* which characterizes *Dallas*. The Ewings are very rich people and can afford everything material: luxury homes, splendid clothes, exclusive dinners, expensive presents, etc.

This wealth does not, however, seem to have many fundamental consequences for the general plot structure of *Dallas* as soap opera: here money has more of an *instrumental* function for the composition of conflict and agony. Money as such is never the source of agony in *Dallas*: rather the ease with which millions of dollars are thrown about gives an extra sensational and bombastic dimension to the interpersonal conflicts with which *Dallas* is preoccupied. It is therefore questionable whether the glamorous *mise-en-scène* does primarily fulfil a *narrative* function, as expressed in the phrase 'money can't buy happiness', which according to some critics is the ideological message of programmes like *Dallas*. Such an explanation ignores the fact that the visual excess of *Dallas* can also produce meanings which are relatively independent of the narrative. The sun-drenched prairie around Southfork, the luxurious swimming pool, the tall, spacious office buildings, the chic restaurants and the elegant women and handsome men – they seem rather to belong to the optimistic image world of advertising, an optimism that does not fit in with the pessimistic world of soap opera, so that the *mise-en-scène* in itself produces a chronic contradiction. It intensifies in this way the claustrophobic sphere of the closed community in which the characters live, in which hysteria can break out any moment, but is also curbed time and again. For in *Dallas* life always goes on normally, whatever happens.

The melodramatic imagination

It is thus the combination of melodramatic elements and the narrative structure of soap opera that evokes a tragic structure of feeling. This tragic structure of feeling does not, however, consist of being bowed down by the Great Tragedy of Man, as is expressed, for example, in classical Greek tragedy, but of a half-conscious realization of the tragic side of ordinary everyday life. Not high-flown *Weltschmerz*, but a completely pedestrian form of suffering. In Newcomb's words, it is a matter here of the simple idea that survival is 'complicated by ambiguity and blurred with pain even in its most sought-after accomplishments'.[43]

But I have said earlier that the tragic structure of feeling, which is inscribed in the meaning-structure of *Dallas*, will not automatically and obviously agree with the meanings viewers will apply to *Dallas*. That will only happen if they are sensitive to it. In other words, the tragic structure of feeling suggested by *Dallas* will only make sense if one can and will project oneself into, i.e. recognize, a *melodramatic imagination*. Viewers must therefore have a certain cultural competence or orientation to understand and evaluate *Dallas* in a melodramatic way. As Charlotte Brunsdon has so aptly put it: 'Just as a Godard film requires the possession of certain forms of cultural capital on the part of the audience to "make sense" [. . .] so too does [. . .] soap opera.'[44] In the case of *Dallas*, the melodramatic imagination seems central to that cultural orientation.

The melodramatic imagination is characterized by Peter Brooks as a type of imagination in which a (semi-desperate) attempt is made 'to bring into the drama of man's quotidian existence the higher drama of moral forces'.[45] The melodramatic imagination should be regarded as a psychological strategy to overcome the material meaninglessness of everyday existence, in which routine and habit prevail in human relationships as much as elsewhere. In other words it is a matter of making 'the world we inhabit one charged with meaning, one in which interpersonal relations are not merely contacts of the flesh, but encounters that must be carefully nurtured, judged, handled as if they mattered'.[46] The melodramatic imagination is therefore the expression of a refusal, or inability, to accept insignificant everyday life as banal and meaningless, and is born of a vague, inarticulate dissatisfaction with existence here and now. This then is the tragic structure of feeling: it is not about the great suffering which plays such a prominent role in the history of humankind and which is generally known as human tragedy – the sufferings of war, concentration camps, famine, etc. – but is rather about what is usually not acknowledged as tragic at all and for that very reason is so difficult to communicate. There are no words for the ordinary pain of living of ordinary people in the modern welfare state, for the vague sense of loss, except in half-ironic, half-resigned phrases such as: 'You win some, you lose some.' By making that ordinariness something special and meaningful in the imagination, that sense of loss can – at least for a time – be removed. It is in this world of the imagination that watching melodramatic soap operas like *Dallas* can be pleasurable: *Dallas* offers a starting point for the melodramatic imagination, nourishes it, makes it concrete.

We may wonder about the social and historical roots of the melodramatic imagination. No single form of imagination, as a way in which the everyday, practical consciousness makes sense of and accounts for the living experiences it is confronted with, just appears out of the blue. To which cultural-historical circumstances does the melodramatic imagination form a fantasmatic answer? Here we can only go into this question briefly.

Peter Brooks connects the melodramatic imagination to the fragmented character of modern society, in which no single system of values is capable any longer of functioning as the binding element for the great variety of events and impressions. The melodramatic is, he says, 'a form of the tragic [. . .] for a world in which there is no longer a tenable idea of the sacred'.[47] In a life in which every immanent meaning is constantly questioned and in which traditions no longer have a firm hold, a need exists for reassurance that life can in fact have meaning and therefore life is worth the trouble, in spite of all appearances to the contrary. According to Brooks the explanation can also be found here for the tendency to sentimental exaggeration which is so characteristic of melodrama. It is as though the melodramatic imagination must impress itself so emphatically because what it wants to express is so uncertain, so difficult to grasp, and therefore too so difficult to justify. When the meaning of life threatens to elude us, the 'larger than life' emotions of the melodramatic imagination offer an anchor.

Other authors have ascribed a specific function to the serial as fiction form on the basis of such considerations. The French semiologist Violette Morin points out, for example, that the popularity of the television serial could derive from the fact that the life depicted in it seems to proceed *more slowly* than real life. According to her this effect is achieved by cramming each scene with meaning, even when it is not directly of interest for the continuance of the narrative: 'People eat, talk, walk about in a TV serial in tune with the rhythm of a constant semantic "braking"; as if they were afraid to be happy at living, as if they were more slow, more cautious than in real life and at all events more healthy in their attitude to the pace of life than everyday existence.'[48] According to Morin, this slow-motion idea of life responds to a desire to slow down, to put the brakes on the hasty nature of modern life. We could conclude from this that the serial form is an extremely suitable vehicle for the melodramatic imagination, because in itself it ascribes more meaning to everyday things than is usual in real life.

But such explanations, in which the melodramatic imagination is linked to the characteristics of modern society, are not specific enough. They take into consideration solely some general, formal characteristics of modern daily life, such as the fragmenting of experience, the transitory nature of time and the break with tradition, and therefore abstract from the socio-cultural differences between the living conditions of different groups of people. It is, however, precisely the concrete, practical living situations of people which demand psychological assimilation and which form the raw material for imagination and fantasy. Not everyone living in an urban, industrialized society will be equally sensitive to the melodramatic imagination. The routes followed by people's imaginative strategies are formed during the course of their personal and subcultural histories and slowly rub through, as it were, into their practical consciousness.

If, as is said of soap opera, it is a 'woman's genre' because it is mainly women who like watching it, then that would suggest that it is mainly women who are susceptible to the melodramatic imagination, a type of imagination which appears to express mainly a rather passive, fatalistic and individualistic reaction to a vague feeling of powerlessness and unease. This 'susceptibility', however, has not so much to do with the material social situation of women (housewives) – this would imply a sociological reductionism – as with the way they have become accustomed to facing situations psychologically and emotionally. The ideologically dominant association of the 'women's area' with a concern for the private sphere and with the caring function is an important determining factor in this, for example.[49]

Moreover, we must not overrate the role of the melodramatic imagination in everyday consciousness. Commonsense thinking is not one-dimensional. On the contrary, it is of a very heterogeneous nature.[50] And there are many other ways in which experiences can be lived and assimilated: a melodramatic manner of perceiving the world can alternate with a humorous, romantic, rebellious or other imaginative strategy. The sense of the melodramatic, the tragic structure of feeling, surfaces only occasionally, often cutting in on a sober acceptance of daily existence. Mostly, too, people only experience melodramatic *moments*. Such a moment can, for example, occur when someone is watching *Dallas*. Then *Dallas* is pleasurable because it makes the melodramatic imagination present and palpable.

Of course this does not mean that there are no other ways of experiencing pleasure from *Dallas*. Viewers can also read it in a completely different way; they can attend to other aspects of the text and respond to them: the ingenious way in which the plots are intertwined, the mythical Western-elements, the technical discussions on oil, J.R.'s venomous humour, and so on. *Dallas* offers points of contact for many types of imagination.

In conclusion, then, we can say that the pleasure of *Dallas* consists in the recognition of ideas that fit in with the viewers' imaginative world. They can 'lose' themselves in *Dallas* because the programme symbolizes a structure of feeling which connects up with one of the ways in which they encounter life. And in so far as the imagination is an essential component of our psychological world, the pleasure of *Dallas* – as a historically specific symbolizing of that imagination – is not a *compensation* for the presumed drabness of daily life, nor a *flight* from it, but a *dimension* of it. For only through the imagination, which is always subjective, is the 'objective reality' assimilated: a life without imagination does not exist.

Pleasure and theory

But the above is a theoretical construction. And theoretical constructions by definition never coincide with immediate experience: they can only shed light on that experience in a onesided way. The capricious and contradictory nature of experience is nullified by this.

As immediate experience, pleasure in *Dallas* is a more or less 'spontaneous' phenomenon: a person enjoys watching it, or otherwise, in some way or other. Experiencing pleasure is not a conscious, directed activity (although one can strive for it), but something that 'happens', something which comes over the viewer according to his or her feelings. The experience is diffuse, bound to time and context, heterogeneous: so much is going on in the viewer's head.

In analysing the pleasure of *Dallas* we have started with the premise that the programme is a text with a specific structure. Pleasure is then connected with the way in which viewers read the text from a specific subject-position. But generally viewers do not approach *Dallas* as text. For them watching it is first and foremost a *practice*. Certainly, in this practice the *Dallas* text occupies a central place, but the practice itself comprises more than that. Therefore it is somewhat misleading – or at any rate inadequate – to deduce the pleasure of *Dallas* totally from its characteristics as text. Watching *Dallas*, just like watching television in general, is a cultural practice which has much of the nature of a habit: it is directly available, casual and free. And a habit is always difficult to explain in intellectual terms, because it feels so natural and self-evident.

A theoretical construction has the character and the effect here, then, of a rationalization. And is it not a fact that we can talk of the experience of pleasure only by means of rationalizations? Pleasure eludes our rational consciousness. This applies not only for theoreticians who want to explain this pleasure, but also for the 'witnesses' or 'reporters' of pleasure, on which the theoreticians base their explanations. It seems as though the letter-writers – my 'reporters' – realize that. Some of them do their very best to express in words why they like watching *Dallas*; they recite reason after reason, in order ultimately, quite unexpectedly, to end their account with expressions of uncertainty such as:

> I don't know, but I like watching it. (Letter 4)

> I don't know exactly what it is but *Dallas* really draws me, there is, I find, a sort of charm radiating from the actors and from the thing itself. I just really love watching it. (Letter 13)

> In a word, there's a bit of everything in that film. Perhaps it's crazy to think so but that's what I see in it. (Letter 16)

> Finally I must just say that, funnily enough, last year I just couldn't stand *Dallas*. Unfortunately I can't say why. (Letter 17)

> I think *Dallas* is a serial for sensitive people, but of course I could be completely wrong. (Letter 18)

> I hope my story has been of some use to you, but I find it really difficult to state exactly why I like *Dallas*. (Letter 20)

> Looking into it more closely, I can imagine you haven't got much from my reaction because it's a bit shallow as an analysis, but I'll send it anyway. (Letter 22)

> Here are some opinions from my brother and from a girl living in our house. They like watching it, amusing and

good-looking people are in it and it is well produced. According to them. My father just says it's shit. I hope this has been some use to you. Unfortunately there's not much you can say about it. (Letter 37)

It is as though the pleasure of *Dallas* eludes the rational consciousness of these letter-writers. They do their utmost to give explanations for that pleasure, but somehow they know that the explanations they can put into words are not the whole story, or even perhaps the 'right' story.

Pleasure is therefore obviously something uncertain and precarious. 'Everyone can testify that the pleasure of the text is not certain: nothing says that this same text will please us a second time; it is a friable pleasure, split by mood, habit, circumstance, a precarious pleasure', writes Roland Barthes.[51] A theoretical (re)construction can therefore never fully comprehend pleasure, because theory makes it something substantial and presumes it to be permanent and static. Nor do we have to agree with Barthes when he asserts that 'we are scientific because we lack subtlety'[52] (scientific subtlety may in fact exist, but this is of a different order from the subtlety of pleasure) to be able to conclude that any theoretical look at pleasure by definition falls short. A conclusion which, however paradoxical it might sound, gives rise to optimism.

3

DALLAS
and the ideology of mass culture

DALLAS and boredom

In the preceding chapters we have seen that the letter-writers who like *Dallas* have difficulty in stating why they do. Many of them finally have to admit that they don't know. This uncertainty is not surprising, as the experience of pleasure is not rationally motivated. On the contrary, pleasure always arises as a spontaneous feeling of well-being. You feel good when you are watching *Dallas* and that makes it enjoyable: no explanation appears to be necessary. People rarely wonder why something is pleasurable to them. Pleasure is one of the things in life regarded as self-evident and which as a rule people don't think about.

Hence, in order to say something about the determinants and structurings of pleasure in *Dallas* one needs to make a theoretical diversion. The letters do not, it is true, contain any straightforward explanations, but they do describe how the letter-writers watch the programme, what aspects of *Dallas* they find most important and most valuable, and what meanings they ascribe to them. I have read the letters 'symptomatically', as it were, to try to find out what it means when the letter-writers say they like *Dallas* and I have reached the conclusion that, at least for *these* fans, it is a sense of emotional realism that appeals to them. More specifically, this realism has to do with the recognition of a tragic structure of feeling, which is felt as 'real' and which makes sense for these viewers. Then by means of an analysis of *Dallas* as a melodramatic soap opera I have set out how this tragic structure of feeling is organized (concretized, made material) in the narrative structure of the serial: the ideological problematic of personal life; the emphasis on the unavoidably contradictory and conflictual character of interpersonal relations, etc., which is reinforced by the fact that the narrative goes on indefinitely.

But what about the letter-writers who don't like *Dallas*? What is their attitude towards this construction of the tragic structure of feeling? The following letter extracts illustrate that the lack of narrative progress, which for *Dallas* fans contributes so much to their pleasure, is for these letter-writers a source of annoyance:

> The stupid thing about the serial, I find, is that in every episode it comes down to the same thing. . . . This serial never changes, every episode is the same. (Letter 32)

> There is absolutely no variation in it. (Letter 33)

> It always revolves around the same thing. One of them has been up to dirty tricks again and someone else is waiting for something and then at the last moment something else happens. Really funny. (Letter 34)

> For *Dallas* you only have to read that little bit in the programme guide and then you can dream up the rest. Quarrels – tears – and it all turns out all right in the end, and on to the next episode. (Letter 36)

Every time I watch it again I'm curious to know what's happening. But then *Dallas* is over and even more questions have arisen. I find that so stupid. . . . And it's much too longwinded. (Letter 37)

The imagination of the tragic structure of feeling as presented in *Dallas* would appear to be completely meaningless for these particular letter-writers. Probably they expect something quite different from a good television serial: their definition of what is enjoyable does not seem to coincide with what *Dallas* has to offer them. One letter-writer states this quite explicitly: 'Well, personally I'd rather watch Roald Dahl, because when you think "now such and such is going to happen" you know that you're going to be wrong because you can never predict it' (Letter 36). The 'longwinded' narrative structure of *Dallas*, its 'indefinitely expandable middle' and the consequent lack of progress, is therefore not a source of enjoyment for these letter-writers, but of boredom.

So even among the letter-writers who don't like the programme we encounter references to aspects of its textual structure. But for them these references are markers to an experience of irritation, not of pleasure. They *don't* feel good when they are watching *Dallas*. Boredom and irritation are also feelings which arise quite spontaneously; for these experiences too we don't generally look for causal explanations. Only if asked will one wonder what the reasons might be for these negative feelings. Just as with the letter-writers who like *Dallas*, then, it would not be surprising if its critics find it difficult to give a consistent and rational explanation for their feelings of irritation.

But, and this is striking, those who hate *Dallas* betray no trace of the uncertainty we encounter among lovers of the programme. Quite the contrary, they seem to take their dislike so much as a matter of course that they confidently believe in the rationality of their dislike. This confidence can be very clearly read from the tone of the following letter extracts:

I find very little style in it and the story very bad, it is *simply* a commercial success. (Letter 34, my italics)

It really makes me more and more angry. The aim is *simply* to rake in money, loads of money. (Letter 35, idem)

There's *just* nothing in this serial, it has *just* no content and always turns out well. (Letter 33, idem)

And those women always look good and that is disgusting *of course*. (Letter 38, idem)

Words like 'simply', 'just' and 'of course' in these statements indicate that these letter-writers not only have no difficulty in giving their opinion, but also that they are convinced that they are right. They feel they are on firm ground. Why then do these particular letter-writers appear so self-confident in their opinions?

Hating DALLAS

The letters of those who dislike *Dallas* are characterized not only by a positive and self-assured tone, but also by a large measure of fury, annoyance and indignation. These people seem not just to dislike *Dallas*: they get terribly worked up by it. Many of them also make considerable use of strong language in judging the programme, as though to emphasize yet again the logic of their hatred: 'worthless rubbish', 'a stupid serial', 'the biggest nonsense', 'eyewash', 'dreadful', 'annoying', 'ghastly', 'daft', 'ridiculous', 'disgusting', etc.

But these letter-writers don't just resort to emotional expressions of anger and frustration. They often go to some length to supply a rational explanation for their dislike. For example, some justify their aversion by denouncing the *Dallas* story as 'stereotypical', especially where the representation of women is concerned.

The ideal life – big house, swimming pool, big cars, lots of money, etc., etc., occupy the centre of interest. (Letter 35)

I also find it so disgusting that there are those perfect, beautiful women in it who are really servile too. Take Sue Ellen. She acts as though she's very brave and can put up a fight, but she daren't take the step of 'divorce'. What I mean is that in spite of her good intentions she lets people walk over her, because (as J.R. wants) for the outside world they have to form a perfect family.

Then that wife of Bobby's. Recently I saw an episode in which Bobby was busy in some (self-glorifying) political campaign or other. A group of men (omniscient of course) were on a visit to the Ewing office: Bobby asked whether Pamela wouldn't like to put some coffee on. It almost looked as though she was going to refuse, but like a good little girl she did as she was told. Of course the fact that she hesitated was meant to make you think about it too, but just imagine the shocked faces of the men if she had refused. Yuk, yuk. But who knows? This Pamela may start an extramarital affair (I must admit she's very beautiful). That will be something else to smack your lips over.

These are just two examples of the inferior role of the women in *Dallas*. Then I still haven't said anything about that tubby little blonde and that mother who condemns lots of things in her heart but never does anything about it. Love is blind? Or aren't you allowed to criticize your husband? (Letter 31)

Now about *Dallas*. When the serial began I really disliked it because in my eyes the characters in it are totally unreal, certainly the women – in the whole of *Dallas* there's not one ugly woman, and these women always look good and that is disgusting, of course. Then the men. They are one and all successful businessmen and stinking rich. Women crawl to them and act like that the whole time. (Letter 38)

My personal opinion of *Dallas* is that I find it a horribly cheap serial. I do admire it, the way they can work it all out every time, how they can set up the most crazy dramas in a series like that. Every instalment the family members all go bawling on non-stop (only the women, of course, men aren't allowed to cry, apparently). (Letter 36)

Such condemnations levelled at the content of *Dallas* can also be combined with disapproval of the presumed insincere intentions of the producers. *Dallas* is a kind of fraud, these letter-writers find, because it is a commercial product:

> You wrote [. . .] whether we wanted to write to you what we thought of *Dallas*. Well, I want to write to you that I find *Dallas* absolute nonsense. The whole serial is only concerned with money. It's just like *Peyton Place*. That was another load of old rubbish. (Letter 33)

> I find very little style in it and the story very bad, it is simply a commercial success, like lots of serials, not just *Dallas*. (Letter 34)

> It really makes me more and more angry. The aim is simply to rake in money, loads of money. And people try to do that by means of all these things – sex, beautiful people, wealth. And you always have people who fall for it. To get high viewing figures. (Letter 35)

But the most comprehensive and total condemnation of *Dallas* is expressed in this letter extract:

> My opinion of *Dallas*? Well, I'd be glad to give it to you: WORTHLESS RUBBISH. I find it a typical American programme, simple and commercial, role-affirming, deceitful. The thing so many American programmes revolve around is money and sensation. Money never seems to be a problem. Everyone is living in luxury, has fantastic cars and loads of drink. The stories themselves are mostly not very important. You never have to think for a moment: they think for you. (Letter 31)

All these condemnations have the same function. Categories like 'stereotypical' and 'commercial' are not only used in the descriptive sense, but invested with a moral status and emotional charge: they serve as explanations for the writers' dislike of *Dallas*. These explanations sound extremely convincing. But, we might ask, are they really as adequate and balanced as they appear at first sight?

It is not my aim here to cast doubt on the sincerity of the feminist and anticapitalist concerns of these letter-writers. But what can be questioned is whether it is really so logical to connect the experience of displeasure, which must in the first instance be an emotional reaction to watching *Dallas*, so directly with a rationalistic evaluation of it as a cultural product. Even if someone does like watching it, he or she can be aware of the 'commercial' or 'stereotypical' character of the programme. Thus, enjoying *Dallas* does not preclude a political or moral condemnation of its production context or its ideological content. The fact that those who hate the serial do make such a connection indicates that categories like 'commercial' and 'stereotypical' exercise a certain attraction, because using them gives the letter-writers a feeling of security. These categories enable them to legitimize their dislike, make it credible and totally comprehensible. They seem to give these letter-writers the conviction that they are right and allow them an uninhibited display of anger.

And so these categories form a central component of an ideological discourse in which the social significance of forms of popular culture is determined in a particular way. This is the ideology of mass culture. In order to understand the self-confidence of those who hate *Dallas* we need now to investigate this ideology more closely.

The ideology of mass culture

Dallas is not only widely watched, but also widely discussed: a lot is said and written about the programme. These public discourses about *Dallas* provide a framework within which answers can be given to questions such as: what must I think about such a television serial? What arguments can I use to make my opinion plausible? How must I react to people who hold a different opinion? Not all existing discourses, however, are equally capable of formulating satisfactory answers to such questions. Some discourses are more prestigious than others, they sound more logical or convincing, and are more successful in determining the social image of TV programmes like *Dallas*.

In many European countries nowadays there is an official aversion to American television series: they are regarded as a threat to one's own, national culture and as an undermining of high-principled cultural values in general.[1] Against this ideological background, professional intellectuals (television critics, social scientists, politicians) put a lot of energy into creating a consistent and elaborated 'theory' on American television series – a theory which provides a 'scientific' cloak for the aversion. A representative and revealing formulation of this theory comes from the sociology of mass communications:

The most important characteristic of a TV series is that the film content is dependent on its economic marketability. Aiming at a very broad market means that the content must be reduced to universally consumable motifs. This applies in particular to American series which in the United States serve as 'commercial' packaging. [. . .] The commercial character of the TV series hinders the introduction of concrete social and political attitudes, because they might provoke controversies in various groups. [. . .] The film is given a 'universal appeal' character; it deals with familiar, broadly institutionalized ingredients. The necessary ingredients of a successful series include romantic love [. . .] simple patterns of good and evil and the building-up of suspense, climax and relief. [. . .] This reduction to the normal human aspects of existence means that the content is recognizable for a wider audience, but it offers a stereotypical and schematized image of reality. [. . .] In this regard TV series succeed in fulfilling primarily economic functions, and thus in reproducing a bourgeois ideology, without losing their attraction for different sectors of the audience.[2]

As a description of the working method of the commercial, American television industry this account certainly offers some adequate insights, although one might wonder whether such a direct connection exists between the economic conditions under which TV series are produced and their aesthetic and narrative structures. Such crude economic determinism is often criticized in media studies circles. Nevertheless, the core of this theory tends to be accepted as correct. What interests us here, however, is not the correctness or adequacy of the theory itself, but the way in which some of its elements carry over into the way in which American TV series are evaluated. A theory fulfils an ideological function if it fulfils an *emotional* function in people's heads, to which the assertions contained in the theory are subordinated. As Terry Eagleton puts it, 'what *is* important to recognize is that the cognitive structure of an ideological discourse is subordinated to its emotive structure – that such cognitions or miscognitions as it contains are on the whole articulated according to the demands [. . .] of the emotive "intentionality" it embodies.'[3]

Emotionally, then, the above-described theory on American TV series leads to their total rejection and condemnation. They become 'bad objects'. These then are the contours of what I would like to call the 'ideology of mass culture'. In this ideology some cultural forms – mostly very popular cultural products and practices cast in an American mould – are *tout court* labelled 'bad mass culture'. 'Mass culture' is a denigrating term, which arouses definitely negative associations.[4] In opposition to 'bad mass culture' implicitly or explicitly something like 'good culture' is set up. One letter-writer expresses this dichotomization of 'bad' and 'good' culture very clearly:

In *Dallas* no attention at all is paid to any realistic problems in this world, the problems of ordinary people, whereas even in America social equality is a long way off. [. . .] I mean, I'd rather read a good book or watch a programme like *Koot en Bie* [a high-brow Dutch satirical programme]. (Letter 31)

So dominant is this ideology of mass culture where the judging of American TV series is concerned that the chairman of the Dutch Broadcasting Foundation, Eric Jurgens, can say without any hesitation: 'The Dutch broadcasting organizations *of course* don't exist primarily to broadcast *Dallas*. [. . .] No *one* can maintain that these American series are of a high standard as regards content. They are at most cleverly made.'[5] The ideology of mass culture takes on here the status of Absolute Truth. Judgement is passed, no doubts allowed.

The emotional attraction of the ideology of mass culture, however, is not confined to the select circle of professional intellectuals. As we have seen, the letter-writers who dislike *Dallas* also all too easily reach for its categories. Apparently the ideology of mass culture has such a monopoly on the judging of a phenomenon like *Dallas* that it supplies ready-made conceptions, as it were, which sound self-evident and can be used without any strain or hesitation. The dominance of the ideology of mass culture apparently even extends to the common-sense of everyday thinking: for ordinary people too it appears to offer a credible framework of interpretation for judging cultural forms like *Dallas*.

It therefore looks as though the letter-writers who hate *Dallas* have adopted the ideology of mass culture as a guideline for its rejection. Because of this the border between individual experience and social ideology tends to become blurred: the way in which these letter-writers watch *Dallas* is described in terms of the ideologically dominant status of *Dallas* as 'mass culture'. The ideology of mass culture therefore not only offers a (negative) label for the programme itself, but also serves as a mould for the way in which a large number of haters of *Dallas* account for their displeasure. To put it briefly, their reasoning boils down to this: '*Dallas* is obviously bad because it's mass culture, and that's why I dislike it.' And so the ideology of mass culture fulfils a comforting and reassuring role: it makes a search for more detailed and personal explanations super-fluous, because it provides a finished explanatory model that convinces, sounds logical and radiates legitimacy.

Hating *Dallas* need not, however, necessarily coincide with subscribing to the ideology of mass culture. Other factors may be responsible for the fact that one is not attracted to the television serial itself. The letters from those who dislike it, however, are so structured by the schemas of this ideology that they offer us little insight into the way in which they watch the programme, which meanings they attach to it, etc. Hence, despite the confidence of their expressed opinions, it remains even more puzzling why some letter-writers don't like *Dallas* than why its fans do.

The ironical viewing attitude

But not all letter-writers who have adopted the ideology of mass culture seem to dislike *Dallas*. On the contrary, some of them state explicitly that they are fond of it, while at the same time employing the norms and judgements the ideology pre-scribes. How is this possible? It seems somewhat contradictory to regard *Dallas* as a 'bad object' on the one hand, but on the other to experience pleasure in watching it. But if we read the relevant letters carefully, it emerges that this apparent contra-diction is resolved in an ingenious manner. How? Let me give an example.

> *Dallas*. . . . God, don't talk to me about it. I'm just hooked on it! But you wouldn't believe the number of people who say to me, 'Oh, I thought you were against capitalism?' I am, but *Dallas* is just so tremendously exaggerated, it has nothing to do with capitalists any more, it's just sheer artistry to make up such nonsense. (Letter 25)

It is clear how this letter-writer 'solves' the contradiction between the moral of the ideology of mass culture and experiencing pleasure in *Dallas*: with mockery and irony. One group of letter-writers seems to make *Dallas* the object of derision. They assume an ironic stance when watching it, an attitude they refer to in their letters at length and with obvious pleasure. An important element of this ironical viewing attitude is the supplying of commentary. According to Michel Foucault commentary is a type of discourse that has the aim of dominating the object:[6] by supplying commentary to something one affirms a superior relation to that object. Thus *Dallas* too is 'dominated' by the mocking commentary of these viewers, 'put in the corner'. Two 'ardent *Dallas* watchers', as they call themselves, tell us how this can be done:

> We never miss this programme for a single week and sit glued to the box, like two flies to a treacle-pot. At first we watched out of pure curiosity, now because we're hooked on it. Mostly we watch with a group of people and we laugh, scream and roar. . . . We ourselves have given a bit of our own flavour (to this programme) such as changing the names. For example Pamela = Memmela. Miss Ellie = Miss Lellie. Sue Ellen = Sod Ellen, etc. We even have a notice-board in the house devoted to the *Dallas* characters. And if one of us can't watch, then a written report of it is drawn up. This board is also richly illustrated. (Letter 28)

Commenting on *Dallas* has here become a ritual. Apparently these letter-writers don't enjoy *Dallas* itself at all, what they seem to enjoy is the irony they bring to bear on it. According to Freud, irony is based on the mechanism of inversion:

> Its essence lies in saying the opposite of what one intends to convey to the other person, but in sparing him contradiction by making him understand – by one's tone of voice, by some accompanying gesture, or (where writing is concerned) by small stylistic indications – that one means the opposite of what one says.[7]

We could add to this that the effect of irony need not necessarily arise through an inversion of the meaning of words, but can also be realized through an inversion of the meaning of an object. Thus, through a mocking commentary *Dallas* is transformed from a seriously intended melodrama to the reverse: a comedy to be laughed at. Ironizing viewers therefore do not take the text as it presents itself, but invert its preferred meaning through their ironic commentary. This can provide brilliant constructions:

> In some sense this serial is a lot like *Soap!* but less satirical. (Letter 29)

> *Dallas* is sensitive and ludicrous. Another of our favourite programmes is *Soap!* (Letter 30)

It is marvellous that these letter-writers connect up *Dallas* with *Soap!* of all things. *Soap!* is a comedy serial which is an explicit parody of soap operas, exaggerating the melodramatic appeal to emotionality and sentimentality to the point of ridicule. Putting *Dallas* and *Soap!* in the same category, as these letter-writers do, is certainly no accident; such a comparison reveals the functioning of and only makes sense from a certain ideological position. The ideology of mass culture is extremely suitable as a foundation for such a position, because the ideology of mass culture regards *Dallas* by definition as a 'bad object' and therefore turns it into an easy subject for mockery and parody.

But it would be too simple to make that ideology the only responsible determinant of an ironic stance towards *Dallas*. Some forms of mass culture are more easily available to an ironic attitude than others. Melodramatic soap operas are an extremely vulnerable genre here: melodrama stands or falls by the degree to which it can whip up passion, sentiment, despair and drama and still carry the viewers along. In other words, the melodramatic effect only works if the viewer identifies with the excessive world of the soap opera. If that is not the case and the viewer feels an outsider to this world, then the melodramatic enlargement of emotions becomes completely senseless and laughable. Melodramatic soap operas are therefore an easy prey for irony: any relativizing is disastrous for melodrama.

However, the ironic viewing attitude makes a reconciliation possible between the rules of the ideology of mass culture ('I must find *Dallas* bad') and the experiencing of pleasure ('I find *Dallas* amusing *because* it's so bad'). As these letter-writers put it:

> My feelings are mostly very superior, such as: what a lot of idiots. And I can laugh at it. Often too I find it over-sentimental. One thing in its favour: It's never dull. (Letter 29)

> As you may notice I watch it a lot, and (you may find this sounds a bit big-headed) I find it amusing precisely because it's so ghastly (if you know what I mean). If, for example, I had had to play Miss Ellie's role, when her breast is amputated, I would really kill myself laughing, with that slobbering Jock hanging over me full of good intentions. (Letter 36)

By ironizing commentary a distance is created from the reality represented in *Dallas*. In this way those who subscribe to the norms of the ideology of mass culture can like *Dallas*. Irony then comes to lead its own life and this viewing attitude becomes a necessary condition for experiencing pleasure in the first place. Thus the conflict disappears between the norms of the ideology of mass culture and liking *Dallas*: ironizing, i.e. creating a distance between oneself and *Dallas* as 'bad object', *is* the way in which one likes *Dallas*. This is, for example, the case for the 'ardent *Dallas* watchers' I quoted above. But the viewing attitude of the following letter-writer is also determined to a large degree by the exorcizing power of the ironic commentary:

> Why does a person watch *Dallas* and in my case, why does a serious, intelligent feminist like watching *Dallas*? It releases

primitive feelings in me. I go dizzy, hate, love, loathe, feel disgusted, condemn and often dash away a tear. Personally I keep aloof from Mills and Boon, but I'm ready to play truant from evening school for *Dallas*. . . . My leisure reading consists 90 per cent of feminist books, but when I'm watching *Dallas* with my girl friend and Pamela comes down the stairs wearing a low-necked dress, then we shout wildly: just look at that slut, the way she prances around, she ought to be called Prancela. Bobby is a decent chap, like my eldest brother, and Jock is like my father, so I can hate them intensely too. I can stand Sue Ellen, neurotic as she is, and J.R. laughs just like Wiegel [Dutch right-wing politician] and that has me jumping with rage. Lucy is too beautiful to be true and I don't find Miss Ellie all that marvellous since her breast operation. [. . .] I like to let it all hang out, a sort of group therapy, mostly together with friends. (Letter 24)

The ironic viewing attitude places this viewer in a position to get the better, in a sense, of *Dallas*, to be above it. And in this way, as a 'serious, intelligent feminist', she can allow herself to experience pleasure in *Dallas*. She says in fact: 'Of course *Dallas* is mass culture and therefore bad, but precisely because I am so well aware of that I can really enjoy watching it and poke fun at it.'

The following letter-writer presents her own viewing attitude in the same sort of way:

I watch *Dallas* regularly and I lap it up. All my girl friends watch it, and it's great fun to slate the whole thing. I find the quality rather bad, but it does have a certain attraction. Lots of money, and beautiful people, good and bad clearly distinguished. It's just as much fun to read a gossip magazine. Nothing sticks. You don't think any more about it, but it's fun. [. . .] The same improbable things happen as in romantic fiction. Insidious illnesses, true love, etc. (Letter 26)

And she ends her letter as follows: 'It's wonderful to watch it but sometimes I do need a realistic book or a good film, not to fall into sentimental despair.'

Here again we have the well-known opposition between 'good culture' and 'bad culture': although this letter-writer does not find 'mass culture' 'bad' in the sense that she dislikes it, indeed she can enjoy it, that enjoyment is in her view a completely different, less high-principled sort of enjoyment than that of 'good culture'.

Just as for the letter-writers who dislike *Dallas*, for these ironizing fans the ideology of mass culture has become common sense: for them too it is self-evident that *Dallas* is 'bad mass culture'. But the very weapon of irony makes it unnecessary for them to suppress the pleasure that watching *Dallas* can nevertheless arouse; irony enables them to enjoy it without suffering pangs of conscience. The dismissive norms of the ideology of mass culture are smoothly integrated in the ironic viewing attitude.

We have seen earlier that those who hate *Dallas* have little difficulty in giving reasons for their dislike: they can always draw on the instant judgements of the ideology of mass culture. However, the ironic fans are in a certain sense on even stronger ground. While liking *Dallas* ironically leads to euphoria and merriment, as we have seen, disliking *Dallas* is accompanied by anger and annoyance. And these are not nice feelings. Hence those who dislike *Dallas* run the risk of a conflict of feelings if, *in spite of this*, they cannot escape its seduction, i.e. if they continue to watch. This can lead to almost tragi-comic ups and downs, as this letter-writer relates:

When the serial started I disliked it intensely. [. . .] I myself started watching the serial because I spent a lot of time in the home of people, the husband of whom was from America and the serial made him think a lot about home. So I watched a few episodes because I was forced to in a way and that's now for me the only reason I watch it. I just want to see how it turns out. The fact is that every time the disasters overlap, so I'm sitting in front of the box and now I never miss a single episode. Fortunately it's on late in the evening so before that I can do some sport or something. I must also add that in every episode there are some things that really annoy me. (Letter 38)

So disliking *Dallas* is certainly not an experience without its ambivalences!

Loving DALLAS

But what about those who 'really' like *Dallas*? How do they relate to the ideology of mass culture?

Ideologies organize not only the ideas and images people make of reality, they also enable people to form an image of themselves and thus to occupy a position in the world. Through ideologies people acquire an identity, they become subjects with their own convictions, their own will, their own preferences. So, an individual living in the ideology of mass culture may qualify him or herself as, for example, 'a person of taste', 'a cultural expert' or 'someone who is not seduced by the cheap tricks of the commercial culture industry'. In addition to an image of oneself, however, an ideology also offers an image of others. Not only does one's own identity take on form in this way, but the ideology serves also to outline the identity of other people. As Göran Therborn puts it, 'in one's subjection to and qualification for a particular position, one becomes aware of the difference between oneself and others'.[8] Thus a dividing line is drawn by the ideology of mass culture between the 'person of taste', the 'cultural expert', etc. and those who, according to this ideology, are not such. Or to be more specific, between those who do recognize *Dallas* as 'bad mass culture' and those who do not.

One *Dallas*-hater thus tries to distance herself from those who like *Dallas*:

I don't understand either why so many people watch it, as there are lots of people who find it a serious matter if they have to miss a week. At school you really notice it when you turn up on Wednesday morning then it's, 'Did you see *Dallas*, wasn't it fabulous?' Now and then I get really annoyed, because I find it just a waste of time watching it. [. . .] Then you hear them saying that they had tears in their eyes when something happened to someone in the film, and I just can't understand it. At home they usually turn it on too, but then I always go off to bed. (Letter 33)

She outlines the identity of the others, those who like *Dallas*, in a negative way, and with a particular degree of confidence: lovers of *Dallas* are almost declared idiots by this letter-writer! Roughly the same pattern, but in somewhat milder terms, emerges in the following extract: 'Reading through it [her own letter], it's a serial a normal person shouldn't watch, because you feel someone else's sorrow and difficulties. For me that's also the reason why so many people find the serial good' (Letter 38). The image of the others, of those who do not recognize *Dallas* as 'bad mass culture', can be summed up shortly but forcefully from the viewpoint of the ideology of mass culture: 'The aim is simply to rake in money, lots of money. And people try to do that by means of all these things – sex, beautiful people, wealth. *And you always have people who fall for it*' (Letter 35, my italics). The ideology of mass culture therefore definitely does not offer a flattering picture of those who like *Dallas*. They are presented as the opposite of 'persons of taste', 'cultural experts' or 'people who are not seduced by the cheap tricks of the commercial culture industry'. How do lovers of *Dallas* react to this? Do they know that this negative image of them exists and does it worry them at all?

In the small advertisement which the letter-writers replied to, I included the following clause: 'I like watching the TV serial *Dallas* but often get odd reactions to it.' It seems to me that the phrase 'odd reactions' is vague at the very least: from

the context of the advertisement there is no way of knowing
what I meant. Yet various lovers of *Dallas* go explicitly into this
clause in their letters: the words 'odd reactions' seem sufficient
to effect an 'Aha!' experience in some fans.

> I have the same 'problem' as you! When I let drop in front of
> my fellow students (political science) that I do my utmost to
> be able to watch *Dallas* on Tuesday evenings, they look
> incredulous. (Letter 19)

> It always hits me too that people react 'oddly' when you say
> you like watching *Dallas*. I think everyone I know watches it
> but some of my friends get very worked up over this serial
> and even go on about the dangerous effects on the average
> TV viewer. I really don't know what I should think of this.
> (Letter 22)

These extracts lead one to suspect that the rules and judgements of the ideology of mass culture are not unknown to
Dallas fans. What is more, they too seem to respond to this
ideology. But they tend to do so in a completely different way
from those who hate *Dallas* or who love it ironically. 'Really'
loving *Dallas* (without irony) would seem to involve a strained
attitude toward the norms of the ideology of mass culture. And
it is this strained relationship which the fans have to try to
resolve.

In contrast to the haters and ironic lovers, who, as we have
seen, express their attitude to the ideology of mass culture in a
rather uniform and unconflicting way, the 'real' fans use very
divergent strategies to come to terms with its norms. One
strategy is to take over and internalize the judgements of the
ideology of mass culture itself:

> I just wanted to react to your advertisement concerning
> *Dallas*. I myself enjoy *Dallas* and the tears roll down when
> something tragic happens in it (in nearly every episode, that
> is). In my circle too people react dismissively to it, they find
> it a typical commercial programme far beneath their

standards. I find you can relax best with a programme like this, although you just have to keep your eye on the kind of influence such a programme can have, it is role-confirming, 'class-confirming', etc., etc. And it's useful too if you think what kind of cheap sentiment really does get to you. (Letter 14)

There is a remarkable about-face in this letter. Instead of stating why she likes *Dallas* so much (which was the question I had put in my advertisement), the letter-writer confines herself to reiterating a reasoning which derives from the ideology of mass culture in answer to the 'dismissive reactions' of her milieu. She doesn't adopt an independent attitude towards this ideology but merely takes over its morals. But whom is she addressing with these morals? Herself? Me (she knows from my advertisement that I like watching *Dallas*)? All *Dallas* fans? It is as though she wants to defend the fact that she enjoys *Dallas* by showing that she is in fact aware of its 'dangers' and 'tricks'; aware, in other words, that *Dallas* is 'bad mass culture'. A similar reasoning can be read in the following letter extract:

> In fact it's a flight from reality. I myself am a realistic person and I know that reality is different. Sometimes too I really enjoy having a good old cry with them. And why not? In this way my other bottled-up emotions find an outlet. (Letter 5)

In other words: watching *Dallas* is all right if you know that it is not realistic and therefore 'bad'.

But a protective strategy can also be employed by actually challenging the ideology of mass culture.

> I am replying to your advertisement as I would like to speak my mind about *Dallas*. I've noticed too that you get funny reactions when you like watching *Dallas* (and I like watching it). Many people find it worthless or without substance. But I think it does have substance. Just think of the saying:

> 'Money can't buy happiness', you can certainly trace that in
> *Dallas*. (Letter 13)

But what has been said here against the ideology of mass
culture remains caught within the categories of that ideology.
Against the opinion 'no substance' (= 'bad') is placed the
alternative opinion 'does have substance' (= 'good'); the
category 'substance' (and thus the difference 'good/bad') is
therefore upheld. This letter-writer 'negotiates' as it were
within the discursive space created by the ideology of mass
culture, she does not situate herself outside it and does not
speak from an opposing ideological position.

But why do these *Dallas* lovers feel the need to defend
themselves against the ideology of mass culture? They obviously
feel under attack. Obviously they can't get round its norms
and judgements, but must stand out against them in order to be
able to like *Dallas* and not to have to disavow that pleasure. But
it is never pleasant to be manoeuvred into a defensive position:
it shows weakness. To have to defend oneself is nearly always
coupled with a feeling of unease.

> You are right in saying that you often get these strange
> reactions. Such as 'So you like watching cheap mass enter-
> tainment, eh?' Yes, I watch it and I'm not ashamed of it. But I
> do try to defend my motivation tooth and nail. (Letter 7)

'Tooth and nail'; the pent-up intensity of this expression
reveals the strong desire of this letter-writer to defend herself
and to justify herself, in spite of her contention that she 'is not
ashamed of it'.

And another letter-writer says:

> Oh well, I'm one of those people who sit in front of the box
> every Tuesday for the *Dallas* programme, actually to my
> own amazement. . . . I must honestly confess that I do like
> watching the serial now. By 'confess' I mean this: at first I felt
> a bit guilty about the fact that I had gone mad on such a

cheap serial without any morals. Now I look at it rather differently. (Letter 11)

'To my own amazement', she writes, in other words 'I hadn't thought it possible'. Her feeling of guilt arises precisely because she has not escaped the power of conviction of the ideology of mass culture, from the branding of *Dallas* as a 'cheap serial without any morals'.

Finally, yet another defence mechanism against the ideology of mass culture is possible. That is, strangely enough, irony again. But in this case irony is not integrated so unproblematically in the experience of watching *Dallas* as in the case of the ironic fans we encountered earlier. On the contrary, here irony is an expression of a conflicting viewing experience. One letter-writer has put this psychological conflict clearly into words. In her account there is an uncomfortable mixture of 'really' liking *Dallas* and an ironic viewing attitude:

Just like you I often get odd reactions when I say that at the moment *Dallas* is my favourite TV programme. [. . .] I get carried along intensely with what is happening on TV. I find most figures in the serial horrible, except Miss Ellie. The worst thing I find is how they treat one another. I also find them particularly ugly. Jock because he doesn't have an aesthetically justifiable head, Pamela because she has to seem so smart, I find that 'common'. I can't stand it that everyone (in the serial) finds her sexy when she looks like Dolly Parton with those breasts. Sue Ellen is really pathetic, she looks marvellously ravaged by all that drink. J.R. needs no explanation. He keeps my interest because I always have the feeling that one day that wooden mask is going to drop. Bobby I find just a stupid drip, I always call him 'Aqualung' (his former role in a series). They are a sad lot, so honest, stinking rich, they want to seem perfect but (fortunately for us!) none of them is perfect (even Miss Ellie has breast cancer, and that cowboy Ray, whom I've really fallen for, is always running into trouble). (Letter 23)

The distance from the *Dallas* characters is great for this letter-writer – witness the annihilating judgement that she passes so ironically on them. Nevertheless her account is imbued with a kind of intimacy which betrays a great involvement in the serial ('I get carried along intensely' . . ., 'I can't stand it' . . ., 'I am interested in him' . . ., 'whom I've really fallen for'). The detached irony on the one hand and the intimate involvement on the other appear difficult to reconcile. So it emerges from further on in her letter that irony gains the upper hand when watching *Dallas* is a social occasion:

> I notice that I use *Dallas* as a peg for thinking about what I find good and bad in my relations with others. I notice this in particular *when I'm watching with a group of people* because then we usually can't keep our mouths shut; we shout disgraceful! and bastard! and bitch! (sorry, but emotions really run high!). We also sometimes try to get an idea of how the Ewings are all doing. Sue Ellen has postnatal depression and that's why she is so against her baby. Pamela is actually very nice and suffers because of Sue Ellen's jealousy. J.R. is just a big scaredy-cat, you can see that from that uncertain little laugh of his. (Letter 23, my italics)

The ironic commentaries are presented here as a *social* practice. This is confirmed by the sudden transition from the use of 'I' to 'we' in this extract. Is it perhaps true to say that the need to emphasize an ironic attitude to viewing, thereby creating a distance from *Dallas*, is aroused in this letter-writer by the social control emanating from an ideological climate in which 'really' liking the programme is almost taboo? In any case intimacy returns further on in the letter as soon as she is talking again in terms of 'I'. And the irony then disappears into the background.

> Actually they are all a bit stupid. And oversensational. Affected and genuinely American (money-appearance-relationship-maniacs – family and nation! etc.). I know all

this very well. And yet. . . . The Ewings go through a lot more than I do. They seem to have a richer emotional life. Everyone knows them in Dallas. Sometimes they run into trouble, but they have a beautiful house and anything else they might want. I find it pleasant to watch. I do realize their ideals of beauty. I look at how their hair is done. I'm very impressed by their brilliant dialogues. Why can't I ever think what to say in a crisis? (Letter 23)

Real love and irony – both determine the way in which this letter-writer relates to *Dallas*. It is clear that they are difficult to reconcile: real love involves identification, whereas irony creates distance. This ambivalent attitude to *Dallas* seems to stem from the fact that on the one hand she accepts the correctness of the ideology of mass culture (at least in a social context), but on the other hand 'really' likes *Dallas* – which is against the rules of this ideology. The irony lies here then in the 'social surface'; it functions, in contrast to the ironizing lovers, for whom irony is interwoven with the way in which they experience pleasure in *Dallas*, as a sort of screen for 'real' love. In other words, irony is here a defence mechanism with which this letter-writer tries to fulfil the social norms set by the ideology of mass culture, while secretly she 'really' likes *Dallas*.

We can draw two conclusions from these examples. First, the fans quoted seem spontaneously, of their own free will, to take the ideology of mass culture into account: they come into contact with it and cannot apparently avoid it. Its norms and prescriptions exert pressure on them, so that they feel the necessity to defend themselves against it. Second, it emerges from their letters that they use a very wide variety of defence strategies: one tries simply to internalize the ideology of mass culture, another tries to negotiate within its discursive framework, and yet another uses surface irony. And so it would appear that there is not one obvious defence strategy *Dallas* fans can use, that there is no clear-cut ideological alternative which can be employed against the ideology of mass culture – at least no alternative that offsets the latter in power of conviction and coherence. And so the letter-writers take refuge in various discursive strategies, none of which, however, is as well worked out and systematic as the discourses of the ideology of mass culture. Fragmentary as they are, these strategies are therefore much more liable to contradictions. In short, these fans do not seem to be able to take up an effective ideological position – an identity – from which they can say in a positive way and independently of the ideology of mass culture: 'I like *Dallas* because . . .'.

But this weak position the fans are in, this lack of a positive ideological basis for legitimizing their love of *Dallas*, has tiresome consequences. Whereas those who hate the programme can present their 'opponents' as, for example, 'cultural barbarians', 'people with no taste' or 'people who let themselves be led astray by the tricks of the commercial culture industry' (thus implying that they themselves are *not*), the fans do not have such a favourable representation to hand. They are not in a position to hit back by forming in their turn an equally negative image of those who dislike *Dallas*; they can only offer resistance to the negative identities that *others* ascribe to them.

According to Therborn, such a psychologically problematic situation is characteristic for subject positions which get the worst of it ideologically. From an ideologically dominant subject position it is possible to stigmatize 'the others' as it were. For the victims of this dominant ideology, however, no such reassuring position is available: they find themselves in a position which, 'while also involving a perception and evaluation of the differences between ego and alter, tends towards resistance to the Other rather than towards forming him or her. This difference is inscribed in the asymmetry of domination.'[9] This situation can have disastrous consequences for *Dallas* fans who feel pushed into a corner by the ideology of mass culture. They can easily be reduced to silence because they can literally find no words to defend themselves. The ground is cut from under them. As one of the letter-writers says: 'I personally find it terrible when I hear people saying they don't like *Dallas*' (Letter 2). As finding it 'terrible' is her only word of defence – apparently nothing else occurred to her – isn't that a form of capitulation?

The ideology of populism

It is wrong, however, to pretend that the ideology of mass culture exercises dictatorial powers. The discourses of this ideology are very important, culturally legitimized organizers of the way in which the social meaning of *Dallas* is constructed, but alternative discourses do exist which offer alternative points of identification for lovers of *Dallas*.

Not all letter-writers who like *Dallas* seem to be troubled by the compelling judgements produced by the ideology of mass culture. Some of them just seem to ignore the 'odd reactions' mentioned in the advertisement text, probably because they do not even know what is meant by it, as this letter-writer indicates: 'I have never yet heard odd reactions – as you wrote in *Viva*. People who didn't watch it had no opinion, and people who did watch it found it nice' (Letter 20).

Apparently this letter-writer lives in a cultural milieu in which the ideology of mass culture has little effect on the way in which people judge patterns of cultural consumption. Hating *Dallas* and loving *Dallas* are in this context positions which are relatively free of the associations evoked by the ideology of mass culture. For this letter-writer, who apparently has no idea of the constraint that the ideology of mass culture exercises on so many other lovers of *Dallas* – 'I am curious about your "odd reactions"', she writes – loving *Dallas* is a pretty carefree affair because she does not seem to be surrounded by the taboo which is created by the ideology of mass culture.

A few other letter-writers do seem to be subject to this atmosphere of taboo, but take up an attitude towards it based on deflating the standards of the ideology of mass culture itself.

That can be achieved by simply refusing to let it bother them: 'When I say I like watching *Dallas*, I often get odd reactions too, but I also like eating at MacDonalds and like poetry a lot, things that get just as strange a reaction' (Letter 24). This letter-writer even flirts a bit with her love for 'mass culture' (MacDonalds!), so that a defence against 'odd reactions' is not necessary.

Other letter-writers again try to undermine the ideology of mass culture by not only resisting the negative identity forced on them, but by retaliating to put the position of those who hate *Dallas* in a negative light. Sometimes they do this in a rudimentary way, for example by turning the tables on those who pretend to loathe the programme: 'I have noticed that among people in my milieu they won't honestly admit that they like watching it, but I do, I really like watching it. [. . .] People often find it sugary but they would like to have a taste of that sugariness just as well, wouldn't they?' (Letter 6).

Against the identity that the ideology of mass culture foists on her, the following *Dallas* fan tries herself to construct an elaborate counter-identity:

> There is no time (in this society) for emotions, which is why you and I often get negative reactions when you're talking about *Dallas*. So various people brand *Dallas* as 'childish', 'too sentimental' or 'slimy'. Perhaps it's also because there are also people who only like action and violence. [. . .] I think *Dallas* is a serial for people with feelings, but I could be wrong of course. (Letter 18)

Another lover of *Dallas* goes even further. In her letter she tries to indicate the social origin of the ideology of mass culture, in order then to make her resistance to it known:

> When I ask for an opinion at school I get the same reactions as you. Does it perhaps have something to do with the fact that I am at grammar school and have my final exams this year? I think so. For you 'have to' follow current affairs

programmes and 'good' films, but who decides for me what *I* find good? I myself of course. (Letter 5)

Her use of language ('I myself of course') reveals a certain degree of pugnacity in her resistance to the norms and opinions of the ideology of mass culture. Here she invokes something like an 'individual right of determination' and betrays a certain allergy to aesthetic standards determined from on high. So she speaks from an ideological position which can be aptly summed up in the well-known saying: 'There's no accounting for taste.'

This is the core of what we can call the ideology of populism, an ideology which is completely opposite to the ideology of mass culture: it arrives at its norms and judgements in a radically opposite way. But it is not impossible for the two ideologies to be united in one person. Thus one ironizing lover characterizes *Dallas* on the one hand as a 'hideously cheap serial' (a statement which fits within the discursive repertoire of the ideology of mass culture), while on the other hand she judges those who dislike *Dallas* from a populist perspective: 'I find the people who react oddly rather ludicrous – they can't do anything about someone's taste. And anyway they might find things pleasant that you just can't stand seeing or listening to' (Letter 36).

This statement clearly illustrates how the populist ideology functions. It is, first and foremost, an anti-ideology: it supplies a subject position from which any attempt to pass judgement on people's aesthetic preferences is *a priori* and by definition rejected, because it is regarded as an unjustified attack on freedom. The populist ideology therefore postulates an identity which is characterized by an appeal to total autonomy: 'But there's just one thing I'd like to make quite clear: please don't let yourself be sat on by other people with their own (odd) ideas (like me)' (Letter 36).

Viewed in this way, the populist position must be particularly attractive for lovers of *Dallas*, because it provides an identity which can be forcefully employed against the codes of the ideology of mass culture. Why is it then that we can trace so little of this position in the letters written by fans?

One explanation lies in the difference in the way both ideologies function. The populist ideology derives its attraction from its direct mode of address, from its ability to produce and ensure immediate certainty.[10] Its discourses are anti-intellectual and consist mainly of no more than short slogans, as the saying 'There's no accounting for taste' makes clear. The populist ideology functions therefore mainly at a *practical* level: it consists of common-sense ideas which are assumed almost 'spontaneously' and unconsciously in people's daily lives. The ideology of mass culture on the other hand is mainly of a *theoretical* nature: its discourses possess great consistency and rationality, they take on the form of more or less elaborate theories. The ideology of mass culture is therefore an intellectual ideology: it tries to win people over by *convincing* them that 'mass culture is bad'.[11]

This difference can explain why in the letters the ideology of mass culture is present in a much more pronounced way than populist ideology. At a theoretical level the latter is the subservient one. It has literally fewer words and less clear-cut 'rational' prescriptions available to defend and legitimize its general attitude that 'there's no accounting for tastes'. For the opposite attitude, namely that 'mass culture is bad', very many arguments lie to hand. So it is not surprising that, if people have to account for taste, for example when they have to give reasons why they like or dislike *Dallas*, they cannot, or only with difficulty, evade the discursive power of the ideology of mass culture. This is why the ideology of mass culture succeeds in ensuring that each category of letter-writers – haters, ironizing lovers, 'real' lovers of *Dallas* – is alive to its norms and judgements and why it seems to brush aside the populist position.

Popular culture, populism and the ideology of mass culture

But the power of the ideology of mass culture is certainly not absolute. Indeed, it is precisely the markedly 'theoretical', discursive nature of this ideology that reveals the limits of its power. Its influence will be mainly restricted to people's opinions and rational consciousness, to the discourses people use when *talking* about culture. These opinions and rationalizations need not, however, necessarily prescribe people's cultural *practices*. It could even be that the dominance of the normative discourses of the ideology of mass culture – as it is expressed in all sorts of social institutions such as education and cultural criticism – has in fact a counter-productive effect on people's practical cultural preferences so that, not through ignorance or lack of knowledge, but out of self-respect they refuse to subject themselves to the prescriptions of the ideology of mass culture or to let their preferences be determined by it.[12] The populist position offers a direct justification for such a refusal, because it rejects altogether any paternalistic distinction between 'good' and 'bad' and dismisses any feeling of guilt or shame over a particular taste. There exists then a cynical dialectic between the intellectual dominance of the ideology of mass culture and the 'spontaneous', practical attraction of the populist ideology. The stricter the standards of the ideology of mass culture are, the more they will be felt as oppressive and the more attractive the populist position will become. This position offers the possibility, contrary to the morals of the ideology of mass culture, of following one's own preferences and enjoying one's own taste.

The commercial culture industry has understood this well. It employs the populist ideology for its own ends by reinforcing the cultural eclecticism underlying it and propagating the idea that indeed there's no accounting for taste, that in other words no objective aesthetic judgements are possible. It sells its products by propagating the idea that everyone has the right to his or her own taste and has the freedom to enjoy pleasure in his or her own way. Perhaps it's not so surprising that the most striking description of the commercial application of the populist position was recently given by Frankie Goes To Hollywood: 'One of the main jobs of the advertisers [. . .] is not so much to sell the product as to give moral permission to have fun without guilt.'[13]

But the populist ideology is applicable not only for the aims and interests of the commercial culture industry. It also links up with what Bourdieu has called the popular 'aesthetic':[14] an aesthetic which is the exact opposite of the bourgeois aesthetic disposition in which an art object is judged according to extremely formal, universalized criteria which are totally devoid of subjective passions and pleasures. In the popular 'aesthetic' on the other hand, no 'judgements of Solomon' are passed on the quality of cultural artefacts. This aesthetic is of an essentially pluralist and conditional nature because it is based on the premise that the significance of a cultural object can differ from person to person and from situation to situation. It is based on an affirmation of the continuity of cultural forms and daily life, and on a deep-rooted desire for participation, and on emotional involvement. In other words, what matters for the popular aesthetic is the recognition of pleasure, and that pleasure is a personal thing. According to Bourdieu the popular aesthetic is deeply anchored in common sense, in the way in which cultural forms in everyday life are approached by ordinary people.

Pleasure, however, is *the* category that is ignored in the ideology of mass culture. In its discourses pleasure seems to be non-existent. Instead it makes things like responsibility, critical distance or aesthetic purity central – moral categories that make pleasure an irrelevant and illegitimate criterion. In this way the ideology of mass culture places itself totally outside the framework of the popular aesthetic, of the way in which popular cultural practices take shape in the routines of daily life. Thus it remains both literally and figuratively caught in the ivory towers of 'theory'.

4

DALLAS
and feminism

Women and DALLAS

As a prime time TV programme, *Dallas* is aimed at a widely heterogeneous, general TV audience, which cannot be defined in terms of a specific class, sex or age. On the contrary, from the perspective of the programme's producers, it is necessary in order to draw as many viewers as possible to make sure that the interest of all members of the (American) family is aroused. In this sense too *Dallas* differs from the daytime soap operas which *are* made with an eye to a specific social audience, namely housewives. This production context inevitably has repercussions on the general narrative content of *Dallas*, because it has to address different spheres of interest and it cannot be restricted to themes and plots which are only attractive for one section of the general audience.

As a result, male characters occupy a much more important place in the fictional world of *Dallas* than in daytime soaps; themes and plots which are traditionally mainly appreciated by men, such as the business world, have a much larger part in the narrative.[1] So it is doubtless no accident that the role of the villain in *Dallas* is occupied by a man (J.R.), instead of a woman, as is mostly the case in daytime soaps.[2] (But it is equally striking that in other prime time soap operas, such as *Dynasty* and *Falcon Crest*, female villains do play a main part.) It is therefore not totally justified to regard *Dallas* as a programme primarily aimed at women, whereas the traditional soap operas in general can indeed be regarded as a 'women's genre'.

None the less, there are indications that *Dallas* is in fact watched and appreciated more by women than by men. For example, in March 1982, when the popularity of *Dallas* had more or less reached its peak in the Netherlands, an average of 52 per cent of the Dutch TV public watched *Dallas* weekly, 69 per cent of whom were women.[3] Moreover, data are available which suggest that women watch *Dallas* in a different way from men. Dutch women seem to be most interested in the mutual relations within the Ewing family and in the love complications in *Dallas*, while they respond much less to the business relations and problems, the cowboy elements and the power and wealth represented. It is not really surprising that for male viewers exactly the opposite is the case.[4] In other words, it is clear that *Dallas* in general means something different for women than for men. And it is precisely those themes that are always dealt with in soap operas that seem to make up the pleasure of *Dallas* for women.

The widespread and continuing popularity of soap operas among women has attracted a lot of attention from feminists. How must the fact that so many women obviously get pleasure from watching soap operas be judged politically from a feminist perspective? Is *Dallas* good or bad for women?

Unfortunately, a lot of mainstream feminist criticism seems to be inspired all too easily by the paternalism of the ideology of mass culture. Especially in the case of the mass media, much energy is spent in obsessively stressing how 'stereotyped', 'role-confirming' and 'anti-emancipatory' the images of women in the media are. This is usually as a result of a content analysis that bears all the limitations of empiricist realism, so that the firm conclusion is reached that such images reflect sexist or patriarchal values. Combined with a mechanistic conception of the effect of such representations on the behaviour and attitudes of women, this leads to a total condemnation of soap operas as reinforcers of the patriarchal status quo and the oppression of women. Women are therefore seen as the passive victims of the deceptive message of soap operas, just as the ideology of mass culture sees the audience as unwitting and pathetic victims of the commercial culture industry. In this context an ideological atmosphere arises containing an almost total dismissal of and hostility towards narrative genres which are very popular among women.

Such a 'monstrous alliance' between feminist criticism and the ideology of mass culture has something self-destructive about it. According to the normative parameters of the ideology of mass culture, 'female' forms of 'mass culture' such as soap operas and popular romances are the lowest of the low, while 'male' genres such as detective and science fiction are considered able to rise above the low level of 'mass culture'. A double standard which reveals a sexist inclination in the ideology of mass culture itself!

But feminist criticism operating along these lines also has more serious drawbacks. Not only is the specifically fictional character of soap operas overlooked, and thus the specific meanings produced in soap opera texts; but the pleasure that female viewers get from programmes like *Dallas* is totally disregarded. As Tania Modleski puts it: 'feminist critics seem to be strenuously disassociating themselves from the seductiveness of the feminine texts'.[5]

Fortunately, however, other views have emerged recently too. The idea that the soap opera is an inherently conservative genre that is not only culturally inferior but also harmful for regular viewers, seems to be gradually losing its self-evident character and its legitimacy. Jane Feuer, for example, in an article in which she analyses the ideological structuring of continuing melodramatic serials like *Dallas* and *Dynasty*,[6] comes to the conclusion that such programmes represent a 'potentially progressive form', precisely because the serial form and the multiple plot structure of these prime time soap operas do not allow for clear-cut ideological positions and constructions. 'Since no action is irreversible, every ideological position may be countered by its opposite. Thus the family dynasty sagas may be read either as critical of the dominant ideology of capitalism or as belonging to it, depending upon the position from which the reader comes at it.'[7] This relative optimism with regard to the possibly progressive effect of prime time soap operas is formulated even more explicitly by Ellen Seiter, who reveals gentle feminist sympathy for the soap opera: 'The importance of small discontinuous narrative units which are never organized by a single patriarchal discourse or main narrative line, which do not build towards an ending or closure of meaning, which in their very complexity cannot give a final ideological word on anything, makes soap opera uniquely "open" to feminist readings.'[8]

Both Feuer and Seiter therefore base their optimism on the relative 'openness' of soap opera narratives, i.e. on the fact that it is impossible to achieve an ideological consensus in soap operas, for the very simple reason that the representation of ambivalence and contradiction forms the very material substance of the genre. This continuing ideological uncertainty creates a certain 'freedom' for viewers to construct their own meanings. It is, then, the viewers and their readings of the text that define the ultimate ideological stance of soap operas. In other words, Feuer and Seiter fasten their hopes on the possibility that viewers will make use of the freedom offered to them, so that the latent progressive potential contained in this narrative form will actually be translated into the manifest production of subversive, feminist meanings.

However, in the absence of any evidence about the way in

which actual readings take place, this reasoning remains abstract. Merely appealing to a progressive potential is a strictly formal matter which is detached from any examination of the concrete social and cultural context in which the programmes function. In this connection it can be relevant to concentrate for a moment on what the letter-writers – mainly women – have told us. As we have seen in previous chapters, the pleasure of *Dallas* for many of them is linked with a tragic structure of feeling that they read from *Dallas*. Such a reading does not seem to be exactly subversive: on the contrary, it fits in totally with the hegemonic consensus constructed in *Dallas* that nothing exists but age-old and eternally insoluble contradiction. Little that is feminist is to be discovered in such an ideological position. If we assume that the tragic structure of feeling is the principal way in which female viewers experience pleasure in *Dallas*, does that mean that Feuer and Seiter's hope is unfounded because any 'feminist potential' of *Dallas* is, alas, not taken up by viewers? Or have we jumped too quickly to this conclusion?

Feminism and the tragic structure of feeling

As a political and cultural movement, feminism is sustained by collective fantasies of a social future in which the oppression of women will have ceased to exist. A future, in other words, in which women's lives will no longer be dominated and hindered by patriarchal structures and sexist practices. All feminist struggles into which women put so much energy in present-day societies are always related in some way or other to this (imaginary) Utopia. Feminist fighting spirit and solidarity today are always motivated by a desire to achieve that distant Utopia, however much that desire is repressed in concrete situations and in the thick of the fight in the deeper layers of day-to-day consciousness.

As a narrative, then, feminist discourse tends to move in the direction of an imagined happy ending. It is the belief in and the commitment to the necessity for this happy end that keeps feminists going. In this sense feminist discourse bears some similarity to the structure of popular romantic fiction, in which the search for a happy ending – for that orgastic moment of 'and they lived happily ever after' – also forms the motor of the narrative. However, the feminist notion of the happy ending has a totally different content from the happy ending of the popular romantic novel, in which the heterosexual, monogamous couple are eternally united in harmony. More strongly still, the way in which this romantic Utopia is achieved is generally deplored because it is seen to be in conflict with the feminist ideal: the heroine of the popular romantic novel wins happiness only after having given up her striving for independence and her resistance to the arrogance and violence of the male hero, and having subjected herself to his authority and paternalist protection.[9] In this sense the narrative of popular romantic fiction is one which asserts that the utopian situation can be realized within the framework of existing, patriarchal power relations between men and women – an imaginary 'solution' totally at odds with the feminist scenario.

But what about soap operas, with their total lack of any sense of progress, a total absence of an outlook on any kind of happy ending? In soap operas it is by definition impossible for the characters to remain happy. A utopian moment is totally absent in soap opera narratives: circumstances and events continually throw up barriers to prevent the capture of that little scrap of happiness for which all the characters are none the less searching. Life is presented as inherently problematic. Unhappiness is the norm, the rule and not the exception. This is the core of the tragic structure of feeling.

As a consequence, women in soap opera can never be simply happy with the positions they occupy. On the contrary, it is often these positions themselves that give rise to many problems and conflicts. This holds pre-eminently for the traditional positions which are ascribed to women in contemporary society. So although motherhood is presented in soap opera as a feminine ideal, at the same time it is a source of constant care and worry. And marriage is not shown to be the blissful region of conjugal harmony but as subject to continual conflict. In a certain sense, then, a tense relationship is expressed in soap operas between the traditional destiny imposed on women by patriarchy and the non-viability of that destiny for women themselves. In other words, it would appear that some points made in feminist analysis of women's oppression are recognized in an intuitive way in soap operas: the contradictions which patriarchy generates are expressed time and again.

But it is precisely the lack of a prospect of a happy ending which makes any solution of these contradictions inconceivable. Women in soap opera never rise above their own problematic positions. On the contrary, they completely identify with them. In spite of all the miseries, they continue to believe in the ideals of patriarchal ideology: whatever the cost, the family must be held together (Miss Ellie); if your marriage breaks down you try again with another man or you become cynical (Sue Ellen); your happiness cannot be complete without children (Pamela). Hence the problems in *Dallas* can never be solved and are essentially cyclical: the patriarchal status quo is non-viable but remains intact.

Viewed in this way, the melodramatic sentimentality of *Dallas* is ideologically motivated by a sense of the essential impossibility of a fundamental alteration in the very structures which should be held responsible for all the trouble and unhappiness. This induces feelings of resignation and fatalism – sentiments which are not exactly conducive to resistance to those structures. From a feminist point of view the *Dallas* women therefore represent 'bad' positions: theirs are positions characterized by fatalism and passivity, while 'good' – feminist – positions should be accompanied by a fighting spirit and activity. It would seem, then, that the tragic structure of feeling is incompatible with a feminist sensibility.

Sue Ellen versus Pamela

Two female positions in *Dallas* are particularly interesting in this respect, because they appear at first sight to be mutually conflicting: those occupied by Sue Ellen and Pamela. It is striking in this context that the opinions of the letter-writers are particularly divided over these two characters. Not all the letter-writers speak about their sympathies and antipathies towards the *Dallas* characters, but some letters indicate that whoever likes Pamela doesn't like Sue Ellen, and vice versa.

> Pamela: a nice girl (I find her a woman of character: she can be nice, but nasty too). Sue Ellen: has had bad luck with J.R., but she makes up for it by being a flirt. I don't like her much. And she's too sharp-tongued. (Letter 3)

> Why do I watch *Dallas* every Tuesday? Mainly because of Pamela and that wonderful love between her and Bobby. When I see those two I feel warmth radiating from them. [. . .] I also find the relationship between Miss Ellie and Jock nice, but I'm scarcely interested at all in J.R. and Sue Ellen. (Letter 8)

> Sue Ellen: just *fantastic*, tremendous how that woman acts, the movements of her mouth, hands, etc. That woman really enters into her role, looking for love, snobbish, in short a real woman. Pamela: a Barbie doll with no feelings, comes over as false and unsympathetic (a waxen robot). (Letter 12)

> Sue Ellen is definitely my favourite. She has a psychologically believable character. As she is, I am myself to a lesser degree ('knocking one's head against a wall once too often') and I want to be (attractive). [. . .] Pamela pouts, and is too sweet. (Letter 17)

> My main person is Sue Ellen (I'm in love with Sue Ellen). She is in fact the only normal person around, especially now she's gone mad. Perhaps that's the secret of *Dallas*. You never know exactly whether anyone is good or bad. Sue Ellen, for example, is she really nice but now and then a bit

disturbed so that she sometimes does something rotten? Pamela, she's always so terribly nice and sweet, I wouldn't trust her an inch. (Letter 23, from a man)

The problematic and conflicting character of Sue Ellen's life stands out most. She tries to compensate for her stormy marriage with J.R. mainly by entering into extramarital relations with other men (Cliff Barnes, Dusty Farlow), and when these fail too she reaches for the bottle. The inner conflicts this causes for her are explicitly expressed in the scenes in which she pours out her heart to her psychiatrist, Doctor Ellby. This Doctor Ellby, by the way, disappeared without trace at a certain moment – he seemed simply not to exist any longer from one episode to the next. But during his presence in *Dallas* he functioned as it were as Sue Ellen's alter ego, he kept telling her that she must believe in her own strength and must begin a new independent life, but Sue Ellen herself does not feel up to this and continues to rely on the help and guidance of a man ('Dusty will get me out of here'). Although she certainly is aware of what makes her unhappy – her dependence on J.R. – she finds no possibility of finally freeing herself from him: she remains with J.R. and at South-fork because she can't go anywhere else.

Pamela's position is different. Certainly at the beginning her marriage to Bobby can definitely be called happy: they really love one another and Bobby is a gentle, understanding man. Of course there are problems: the fact that Pamela can't have children puts a damper on their marital bliss (she has a miscarriage), and when both of them put a lot of energy into their work for a while (Pamela in a fashion business, Bobby in Ewing Oil), it threatens to weaken their marriage. But in Pamela's case the hope remains that finally love will conquer all.

Sue Ellen and Pamela are not close friends. They have little to do with each other and don't pay each other much attention: the major part of their emotional energy is bestowed on the men in their lives. Scenes dealing with the relations between the two women are, true to type, very infrequent in *Dallas*. Yet we do get to see such scenes from time to time. It is, however, striking that the subject of discussion in these scenes is nearly always the same: their common position as Ewing wives.

In one of the scenes the discussion starts because of Miss Ellie's mastectomy. In an earlier scene Sue Ellen has told J.R. that she finds what has happened to Miss Ellie appalling. 'But she will stay alive', J.R. had said to her, as though to reassure her, but she answers: 'Sometimes that is not enough.' In the following dialogue with Pamela it becomes clear exactly what she means by this:

Pamela: You can't handle it, can you?

Sue Ellen: I don't know what you're talking about.

Pamela: I'm talking about Miss Ellie's operation.

Sue Ellen: Can *you*?

Pamela: I don't know, and I hope I don't ever have to know.

Sue Ellen: J.R. fell in love with me because I was a beauty queen . . .

Pamela: There are other things important to a woman besides beauty.

Sue Ellen: What? Brain, charm, personality? You don't believe that for a minute, do you?

Pamela: Yes, I do.

Sue Ellen: Well, I've never met a man yet who thought of brains when he first looked at a woman.

Pamela: Women don't just exist for men, we exist for ourselves first!

Sue Ellen: Not if you're married to a Ewing.

Pamela: Well, I am married to a Ewing.

Sue Ellen: Then open up your eyes! The Ewing men come first, I would have thought you've learned that by now!

Pamela: I think you forget that I'm married to Bobby not J.R.

Sue Ellen: Bobby, J.R., Jock, it doesn't matter. In a couple of years they'll look at you in the same way: as property. And you'd better be wrapped up in a pretty little package!

In another scene in which the two women have a conversation, many months later, they each occupy roughly the same standpoints, although Pamela's marriage at that moment is suffering severely from the fact that Bobby has thrown himself completely into his position as director of Ewing Oil and has therefore alienated himself a little from her. Pamela feels neglected and looks for compensation not only in her own work, but also in a friend, a certain Alex Ward. This Alex makes every attempt to seduce Pamela. Pamela definitely does not appear impassive to this, but as yet she does not want to be unfaithful to Bobby. The discussion with Sue Ellen takes place after Sue Ellen has noticed Pamela in the company of Alex in a restaurant. We are in the living room of Southfork Ranch, where Pamela has just knocked back a stiff drink. At that moment Sue Ellen comes in.

Sue Ellen: It looks like you needed that drink, Pam. I know the difference between problem drinking and drinking for pleasure!

Pamela: Hello, Sue Ellen.

Sue Ellen: Your secret is safe with me, Pam.

Pamela: I see Alex quite often. [. . .] It was a business lunch.

Sue Ellen: Well, I'm not the one to give you advice, but we're both married to Ewing men. It would be easier for you to realize that Ewing women must make their own lives.

Pamela: Well, I've made a life of my own, I work.

Sue Ellen: I'm not talking about work, I'm talking about total lives. The Ewing men are into power first, and affection second.

Pamela: I will never accept the fact that Bobby and J.R. are the same.

Sue Ellen: How can you say that? What was your life like when he was running Ewing Oil?

. . .

Sue Ellen: If J.R. seeks sex and affection somewhere else, so why shouldn't I? And why shouldn't you?

Pamela: Because it's not that way!

Sue Ellen: Pam, I just want you to protect yourself. All Ewing men are the same. [. . .] And for you to survive you have two choices. You can either get out, or you can play by their rules!

At this moment Bobby comes in. He steers towards Pamela and embraces her tenderly. We see a close-up of Pamela, looking over Bobby's shoulder radiantly and triumphantly at Sue Ellen, as though to say: 'You can see we really love one another!' But the last shot of the scene is a lingering close-up of Sue Ellen, looking smilingly after the embracing couple with a look clearly expressing her conviction of the inevitable decline of their love.

Sue Ellen and Pamela share a common social position – that of a (Ewing) wife – but they have very different attitudes towards it. Sue Ellen's cynicism with regard to the male world makes her subject herself recklessly to the norms and rules of that very male world. Pamela on the other hand still believes in the possibility of a harmonious, equal relationship with a man, refuses to acknowledge that there are unbridgeable contradictions and panics when she is actually confronted with them. Sue Ellen's position, then, fits into and expresses to an extreme degree the tragic structure of feeling, while Pamela's position is based on an obstinate denial of it. Indeed, her continuing belief in the Utopia of 'true love' reminds one rather of the structure of feeling borne by the heroine of the popular romantic novel. No wonder that some letter-writers affirm their sympathy for Pamela by projecting on to her the fantasy of the romantic happy ending:

> I really like watching it, and especially Pamela and Bobby because it comes across (in the film) like genuine love, even though it's only a film. (Letter 6)

> If they (the writers) ever write Pamela and Bobby out of the serial then it's over for me. The good relationship between those two is for me the reason for watching. But then, I still firmly believe in 'true love'. (Letter 8)

But within the framework of a melodramatic soap opera like
Dallas Pamela's position is an impossible one. No happy
ending is ever achievable: her hopes will of necessity remain
unfulfilled. So it is not surprising that Sue Ellen's certainty over
the futility of Pamela's dream appears later to be verified. The
estrangement between Pamela and Bobby seems to have been
overcome when they adopt a child, Christopher, but not even
that can save their marriage. The tensions become so acute that
Pamela even decides at a certain moment to leave Bobby and
Southfork and live alone. She begins building up a new life: she
becomes her brother Cliff's business partner and meets a new
man, Mark Graison, whom she does not really love, however.
Bobby continues to haunt her thoughts, although a divorce
seems inevitable. For Sue Ellen too the situation is changed,
although not fundamentally. She does, it is true, succeed in
divorcing J.R., goes to live alone, but quickly gives in to J.R.'s
skilful attempts to win her back. Against her better judgement
she marries him again. This second marriage is an instant
fiasco: J.R.'s sole aim in fact is to ensure that he has an heir
(their little son John Ross) and he is otherwise completely
unchanged. Confronted with this situation, Sue Ellen decides
to abandon all attempts to be happy. . . . During a meeting
between the two women in a park, with happily playing
children in the background, the dilemmas are made clear yet
again.

> *Sue Ellen*: I think it depends on what you want. . . .
> *Pamela*: I want to wipe away the last year, and I want things
>   back the way they were.
> *Sue Ellen*: If only we could wipe away the things that change
>   our lives. Of course, things are much simpler for me than
>   they are for you.
> *Pamela*: Why? We're both married to Ewings.
> *Sue Ellen*: The difference is that you're a strong woman,
>   Pam. I used to think I was, but I know differently now. I
>   need Southfork. On my own, I don't amount to much. As

much as I hate J.R., I really need to be Mrs J. R. Ewing. And I need him to be the father of John Ross. So I guess I just have to lead a married life without a husband.

Pamela: Sue Ellen, there are other ways.

Sue Ellen: Not for me, but for you. . . . You've made your own way of life. Now you're part of Wentworth Industries, you're rich in your own right and you've got Mark Graison out there waiting to marry you. You can never be happy at Southfork again. . . .

Pamela: Sue Ellen, maybe everything you say is true. But what do I do about the fact that I still love Bobby?

Sue Ellen: Sometimes love just isn't enough, Pam. I'm living proof of that.

Sue Ellen is the one who talks most, because she has found a 'solution' to surviving in her terrible situation. She knows that there is no way out for her and accepts things as they are. Pamela however still cannot and will not accept, but is powerless before the overwhelming force of circumstances. She just doesn't know what to do. Which position is more tragic then: the cynical fatalism of Sue Ellen, who has given up all her desires, or the false hope of Pamela, who cannot find an outlet for her desires, no matter how strong they are?

Sue Ellen and Pamela personify two feminine subject-positions which are the result of being trapped in an all-embracing patriarchal structure. Despite the apparent differences between the two, then, in the end both share the same fate. The contradictions of patriarchy are experienced at first hand and even diagnosed, but there is no prospect of change: feminist fantasies are totally absent in *Dallas*.

Pleasure, fantasy and cultural politics

What then about the 'feminist potential' of *Dallas*? What does it mean to get pleasure from *Dallas* by recognizing and identifying with its tragic structure of feeling, as so many female viewers seem to do?

Pleasure has so far not been discussed in this chapter. Yet pleasure is something that concerns many feminists and that is often seen as a problem for a feminist cultural politics. As part of a broader political issue, two questions can be asked concerning pleasure. First, what is the relevance of pleasure for a political project such as feminism? And secondly: what is the political and cultural meaning of the specific forms of pleasure which women find attractive?

There are no simple answers to these questions, but feminists certainly are convinced of the political importance of seeking satisfactory answers. Thus Michèle Barrett wonders: 'How can we widen the purchase of feminist ideas if we cannot understand why so many women read *Woman* and watch *Crossroads*?'[10] The relevance of pleasure is argued here by Barrett in a quite specific way. The understanding of women's existing pleasures, she appears to assert, can be useful for developing a more effective way of spreading feminist consciousness among the mass of women. Precisely how remains unclear for the present, but one positive point of Barrett's argument is that the enormous popularity among women of certain cultural forms is taken seriously. Thus she continues: 'We need to know why the "women's weepies" have an apparently enduring appeal ... we need to examine much more open-mindedly and sympathetically their basis in our consciousness and subjectivity.'[11]

By presenting the problem in this way, Barrett avoids the moralism of the ideology of mass culture in which pleasure in 'mass culture' is regarded as illicit. Women's weepies and all other forms of popular culture for women (such as fashion, lyrical love songs and soap operas) must no longer be simply condemned: we must recognize that they have a positive value and meaning in women's lives. At the same time, however, Barrett does not attempt to fall into the opposite extreme; she does not endorse the populist position in which any pleasure is by definition justified and is above all discussion, because for her the understanding of these traditional pleasures of women is explicitly linked with a feminist aim. It is certainly not the aim to simply glorify those pleasures *because* they are popular among women – which would be a form of deceptive, populist solidarity – but to understand more thoroughly what concerns women today, so that feminists can connect up with it more efficiently. Women fortunately no longer need feel ashamed or guilty if they watch *Dallas*, but at the same time feminists must look for a way of making such pleasures politically productive by situating them in a feminist plan of action.

But it remains unclear what conclusion we must draw from Barrett's argument. How, for example, can the fact that so many women feel attracted to *Dallas* be made politically useful? Does it mean that feminists must make 'feminist soap operas' – whatever they might look like? Or is it a matter of creating contexts in which subversive readings of *Dallas* are promoted, so that the hope that Feuer and Seiter nourish in the 'feminist potential' of soap operas is realized after all?

A serious theoretical problem arises here. This has to do with the danger of an overpoliticizing of pleasure. However much Barrett, for example, tries to approach women's weepies in an open-minded and sympathetic way, her basic premise never-theless remains that its enjoyment is ultimately politically bad for women, because it does not lead to the adoption of feminist ideas. A new antagonism is constructed here: that between the fantasies of powerlessness inscribed in the tragic structure of feeling, and the fantasies of protest and liberation inscribed in the feminist imagination. But what does this antagonism imply? Does experiencing pleasure in fantasies of powerless-ness necessarily lead to political passivity, as the antagonism suggests?

What is at stake here is the relationship between fantasy life, pleasure and socio-political practice and consciousness. In this context it is perhaps of less importance to wonder *why* women's weepies have such enduring appeal, as Barrett would have it, than to ask *what implications* the sentimental pleasure of identification with the tragic structure of feeling has for the way in which women make sense of and evaluate their position in society. And as the enduring popularity of women's weepies even among feminists would indicate, it is very doubtful whether the two are as intimately interrelated as is sometimes assumed. Must we see an imaginary identification with the tragic and masochistic positions of Sue Ellen or Pamela as a form of 'oppression in ourselves', a patriarchal 'remnant' that unfortunately women still have to hark back to because feminism has not yet developed any effective alternatives? Or can such fantasmatic scenarios have a meaning for women which is relatively independent of their political attitudes?

Although political activity certainly comprises a moment of pleasure because it provides one with a sense of positive identity, the project of feminism as a whole is not and never can be based on pleasure alone, because the project itself is impelled by an angry rejection of the existing social order as essentially unpleasurable, and by a projection of pleasure into a (mythical) ideal future. For that reason many feminist fantasies today are not pleasurable, but are linked with feelings of fury, frustration and pain. Political struggle is directed towards removing the distance between an ideal of the future and a given reality, but the harsh conditions in which this struggle must be waged inevitably create tensions in everyday life. Frustrations are always lurking but, from a political perspective, may not lead to giving up that ideal: the struggle must go on. A feeling of discomfort therefore always underlies, and is essential for, any political struggle for a better future, and for two reasons: because of the realization that that future does not yet exist, and because of the realization that a lot of energy has to be invested to bring that future closer.

But it is impossible to live solely with a feeling of discomfort. We cannot wait until the distant Utopia is finally achieved: here and now we must be able to enjoy life – if only to survive. In other words, any uneasiness with the present, with the social situation in which we now find ourselves, must be coupled with an (at least partial) positive acceptance and affirmation of the present. Life must be experienced as being worth the effort, not just because a prospect exists for a better future, but also because the present itself is a potential source of pleasure.

One dimension of life in which the distance between a (pleasurable) absent and an (unpleasurable) present can be eradicated is that of fantasy. Fantasies of the feminist Utopia, for example, can remove the feeling of unease by making the absent ideal present – in the imagination. Here it is not primarily a matter of the content of the fantasy, but mainly of the fact of fantasizing itself: producing and consuming fantasies allows for a play with reality, which can be felt as 'liberating' because it is fictional, not real. In the play of fantasy we can adopt positions and 'try out' those positions, without having to worry about their 'reality value'. In this sense then it is also little to the point to assume that imaginary identifications with the positions of 'cynical fatalism' (Sue Ellen) or 'false hope' (Pamela) would be politically bad because they would lead to pessimism and resignation in real social life. At the level of fantasy we can occupy those positions without having to experience their actual consequences. It may well be, then, that these identifications can be pleasurable, not because they imagine the Utopia to be present, but precisely because they create the possibility of being pessimistic, sentimental or despairing with impunity – feelings which we can scarcely allow ourselves in the battlefield of actual social, political and personal struggles, but which can offer a certain comfort if we are confronted by the contradictions we are living in. It is in this sense that we can interpret Terry Lovell's assertion that 'Soap opera may be [. . .] a context in which women can ambiguously express *both* goodhumoured acceptance of their oppression *and* recognition of that oppression, and some equally goodhumoured protest against it.'[12] But, we must add, this acceptance (just like protest) takes place within the world of fantasy, not outside it. It says nothing about the positions and standpoints that the same women occupy in 'real life'. After all, watching soap operas is never the only thing they do. In other activities, other positions will be (or have to be) assumed.

Fantasy is therefore a fictional area which is relatively cut off and independent. It does not function in place of, but beside, other dimensions of life (social practice, moral or political consciousness). It is a dimension of subjectivity which is a source of pleasure *because* it puts 'reality' in parentheses, because it constructs imaginary solutions for real contradictions which in their fictional simplicity and their simple fictionality step outside the tedious complexity of the existing social relations of dominance and subordination.

It seems therefore impossible to ascertain whether the pleasure of *Dallas* that is based on a recognition of and identification with the tragic structure of feeling is intrinsically progressive or conservative, and therefore politically good or bad – such a question would moreover contain an instrumentalist conception of pleasure, as though pleasure itself doesn't much matter – because that pleasure is first and foremost connected with the *fictional* nature of the positions and solutions which the tragic structure of feeling constructs, not with their ideological content. In terms of *content* the fantasy positions and solutions brought about by the tragic structure of feeling and the melodramatic imagination do seem indeed to incline to conservativism, and of course they can and must also be criticized for this – i.e. in so far as they are conservative representations. The politics of representation does matter. But the fact that we can identify with these positions and solutions when we watch *Dallas* or women's weepies and experience pleasure from them is a completely different issue: it need not imply that we are also bound to take up these positions and solutions in our relations to our loved ones and friends, our work, our political ideals, and so on.

Fiction and fantasy, then, function by making life in the present pleasurable, or at least livable, but this does not by any means exclude radical political activity or consciousness. It does not follow that feminists must not persevere in trying to produce new fantasies and fight for a place for them; at the level of cultural production the main issue of struggle is clear, as many feminist filmmakers, writers and artists have shown. It does, however, mean that, where cultural consumption is concerned, no fixed standard exists for gauging the 'progressiveness' of a fantasy. The personal may be political, but the personal and the political do not always go hand in hand.

Notes

Introduction

1 R. Corliss, 'TV's *Dallas*: Whodunnit?', *Time*, 11 August 1980, p. 63.
2 A. Mattelart, X. Delcourt, M. Mattelart, *International Image Markets*, Comedia, London, 1984, p. 90.
3 ibid., pp. 17–18.
4 Pierre Juneau, 'Audience fragmentation and cultural erosion: a Canadian perspective on the challenge for public broadcasting', *EBU Review*, vol. XXXV, no. 2, March 1984, p. 20.
5 H. Newcomb, 'Texas: A giant state of mind', *Channels of Communication*, April/May 1981, pp. 40–1.
6 I. Ang and M. Simons, Interview with Stuart Hall, *Skrien*, no. 116, March 1982, p. 14.

Chapter 1

1 See also chapter 3 for the function of what I call 'the ideology of mass culture'.
2 Here some titles of the Dutch gossip magazines are listed.
3 It also appears, according to an enquiry carried out by the

Department for Viewing and Listening Research of the Dutch Broadcasting Foundation (May 1982), that only 12 per cent of Dutch adults who regularly watch *Dallas* frequently read something about *Dallas* in a newspaper or magazine; 49 per cent do not do so, 18 per cent seldom and 21 per cent only now and again. This means that only a small overlap exists between watching *Dallas* and reading about things to do with the programme.

4 D. Prokop, *Faszination und Langeweile. Die populären Medien.* Ferd. Enke Verlag, Stuttgart, 1979, p. 1.

5 S. Frith, *Sound Effects. Youth, Leisure and the Politics of Rock 'n' Roll*, Pantheon, New York, 1982, p. 284.

6 Quoted in Ang and Simons, Interview with Stuart Hall, p. 13.

7 Karl Marx (trans. M. Nicolaus) *The Foundations of the Critique of Political Economy*, Penguin, Harmondsworth, 1973.

8 T. Lovell, *Pictures of Reality. Aesthetics, Politics and Pleasure*, BFI, London, 1980, p. 60.

9 P. Bourdieu, 'The aristocracy of culture', *Media, Culture and Society*, vol. 2, no. 3, 1980, pp. 225–54.

10 This is, for example, the main issue for Elihu Katz and Tamar Liebes in their enquiry into the reception of *Dallas* by different sections of the public in Israel. See E. Katz and T. Liebes, 'Once upon a time, in Dallas', *Intermedia*, vol. 12, no. 3, May 1984.

11 Some sociologists emphasize that what we call leisure time is not in fact *free* time at all because the way we spend it (what, when, how) is determined by all sorts of institutions which have pounced on the organization of leisure. This is correct, but it should be added that leisure is in fact really *experienced* as free time: as the opposite of work time. And it cannot be denied that the possibilities of filling leisure time according to one's own ideas, although institutionally limited, are in general greater than at the workplace or at school, where the rules one is subjected to are much more rigid than the 'invisible' rules of how one spends one's leisure time.

12 Except of course for the professional television watchers, the critics, who generally can only grumble about television.

13 There are two television channels in the Netherlands. Research has revealed that only very few viewers – at most around 10 per cent – occasionally watch foreign (German or Belgian) broadcasts. Most viewers have a pronounced preference for the domestic channels.

14 R. Williams, *Television, Technology and Cultural Form*, Fontana, London, 1974, p. 94.

15 Of course this idea is often ideologically misused to justify broad-

casting policy in an easy way and to shrug off appeals to cultural responsibility. But that is beside the point here.

16 Frith, *Sound Effects* . . ., p. 92.

17 For a foundation of this semiological approach to television programmes, see *inter al.* U. Eco, 'Towards a semiotic inquiry into the television message', *Working Papers in Cultural Studies*, no. 2, 1972; and S. Hall, 'Encoding and decoding in the television discourse', CCCS Occasional Stencilled Papers, Birmingham, 1973.

18 See also R. C. Allen, 'On reading soaps: a semiotic primer', in E. Ann Kaplan (ed.), *Regarding Television*, American Film Institute, Los Angeles, 1983.

19 D. Morley, *The 'Nationwide' Audience*, BFI, London, 1980, p. 10.

20 J.-M. Piemme, *La Propagande inavouée*, Union Générale d'Editions, Paris, 1975.

21 ibid., p. 176.

22 ibid., p. 114.

23 'Empiricist' because the basic premise is used that reality can be gathered from the manifestation of the world. Cf. C. MacCabe, 'Theory and film: principles of realism and pleasure', *Screen*, vol. 17, no. 3, 1976, pp. 9–11.

24 R. Williams, *Marxism and Literature*, OUP, Oxford, 1977, p. 97.

25 Piemme, *La Propagande inavouée*, pp. 120–1.

26 C. MacCabe, 'Realism and the cinema: notes on some Brechtian theses', *Screen*, vol. 15, no. 2, 1974; reprinted in part in T. Bennett, S. Boyd-Bowman, C. Mercer, J. Woollacott (eds), *Popular Television and Film*, BFI, London, 1981, pp. 216–35.

27 'While traditional debates about realism have centred on the content and the ability to reflect reality, classic realism should be considered as centrally defined by a certain formal organization of discourses whereby the narrative discourse is placed in a situation of dominance with regard to the other discourses.' C. MacCabe, '*Days of Hope.* A response to Colin MacArthur', in Bennett *et al.* (eds), *Popular Television and Film*, p. 310.

28 MacCabe, 'Theory and film: principles of realism and pleasure', p. 17.

29 I can only deal very briefly here with the Hollywood film conventions. See further D. Bordwell and K. Thompson, *Film Art. An Introduction*, Addison Wesley, Reading, 1980. Also useful is J. Monaco, *How to Read a Film*, OUP, New York/Oxford, 1981 (rev. edn).

30 See also Piemme, *La Propagande inavouée*, 170–1.

31 For a critique of the theory of the classic-realist text, see *inter al.* T. Lovell, *Pictures of Reality*, pp. 84–7; also D. Morley, 'Texts, readers, subjects', in S. Hall, D. Hobson, A. Lowe, P. Willis (eds), *Culture, Media, Language*, Hutchinson, London, 1980, pp. 163–73.

32 The distinction between denotation and connotation is made among others by Roland Barthes in his *Elements of Semiology*, Jonathan Cape, London, 1967. Subsequently various semiologists have contested this distinction, because it suggests a hierarchy between 'literal' and 'figurative' meaning, which does not in fact exist. However, in his *S/Z*, Hill & Wang, New York, 1974/ Jonathan Cape, London, 1975, Barthes defends this distinction if it is a matter of the analysis of what he calls 'the classical text' (as opposed to the 'modern text'). It is in any case important to regard the distinction between denotation and connotation as an analytical difference. See also S. Hall, 'Encoding/Decoding', in Hall *et al.* (eds), *Culture, Media, Language*.

33 R. Barthes, *The Pleasure of the Text*, Hill & Wang, New York, 1975/Jonathan Cape, London, 1976, pp. 11–12.

34 This supposition is not completely correct. There will also be things in *Dallas* the importance of which is so self-evident for faithful viewers that they are no longer aware of it. Thus what is *not* said also plays a role. Here lies one of the limitations adhering to research that uses people's statements as the empirical point of departure.

35 The concept 'structure of feeling' comes from Raymond Williams. See for example his *Marxism and Literature*, pp. 128–35.

36 For a fundamental critique of the way in which the concept 'escape' is used in mass communications theory, see J.-M. Piemme, *La Télévision comme on la parle*, Labor, Brussels, 1978, chapter 4.

Chapter 2

1 For the theoretical problems and consequences of the use of the concept of genre in film theory, see S. Neale, *Genre*, BFI, London, 1980.

2 C. Geraghty, 'The continuous serial: a definition', in R. Dyer (ed.), *Coronation Street*, BFI, London, 1980, p. 10.

3 ibid., pp. 14–15.

4 Todorov, quoted in Geraghty, 'The continuous serial . . .', p. 13.

5 For a history of soap opera, see M. Edmonson and D. Rounds,

The Soaps, Stein & Day, New York, 1973; M. G. Cantor and S. Pingree, *The Soap Opera*, Sage, Beverley Hills, 1983.

6 For the function of soap operas for housewives, see H. Herzog, 'What do we really know about daytime serial listeners?' in P. F. Lazarsfeld and F. N. Stanton (eds), *Radio Research*, Duel, Sloan & Pearce, New York, 1944; D. Hobson, *Crossroads. The Drama of a Soap Opera*, Methuen, London, 1982, chapter 6.

7 Frith, *Sound Effects . . .*, p. 46.

8 See also E. Seiter, 'Men, sex and money in recent family melodramas', *Journal of the University Film and Video Association*, vol. XXXV, no. 1, winter 1983.

9 T. Brooks and E. Marsh, *The Complete Directory to Prime Time TV Shows*, Ballantine, New York, 1981, p. 178.

10 T. Modleski, 'The search for tomorrow in today's soap operas', *Film Quarterly*, fall 1979, p. 12.

11 S. Johnston, 'Crossroads: approaches to popular television fiction', paper read at BFI Summer School 1981, p. 10.

12 G. Swanson, '*Dallas*, part 1', *Framework*, no. 14, spring 1981, p. 62.

13 C. Brunsdon, 'Crossroads: notes on soap opera', *Screen*, vol. 22, no. 4, 1981, p. 34.

14 ibid., p. 34.

15 W. Brakman, in a radio interview, 9 January 1982.

16 D. Thornburn, 'Television melodrama', in R. Adler and D. Cater (eds), *Television as a Cultural Force*, Praeger, New York, 1976, p. 78.

17 See M. Jordan, 'Convention and realism', in Dyer (ed.), *Coronation Street*.

18 H. Newcomb, *TV: The Most Popular Art*, Anchor Books, New York, 1974, p. 137.

19 ibid.

20 T. Elsaesser, 'Tales of sound and fury', *Monogram*, no. 4, 1972, p. 2.

21 ibid., p. 14.

22 S. Sontag, *Illness as Metaphor*, Vintage Books, New York, 1979.

23 M. B. Cassata *et al.*, 'In sickness and in health', *Journal of Communication*, vol. 29, no. 4, autumn 1979, pp. 73–80.

24 Thornburn, 'Television melodrama', p. 83.

25 L. Mulvey, 'Notes on Sirk and melodrama', *Movie*, no. 25, winter 1978, p. 53.

26 Swanson, '*Dallas*, part 1'.

27 See E. Tee, 'Dallas: het gezin van de week', *Skrien*, no. 118, May/June 1982.

28 Swanson, 'Dallas, part 1'.

29 L. Mulvey, 'Sirk and melodrama', *Australian Journal for Screen Theory*, no. 4, 1978, p. 30.

30 Mulvey, 'Notes on Sirk and melodrama', p. 54.

31 ibid.

32 See also J. Feuer, 'Melodrama, serial form and television today', *Screen*, vol. 25, no. 1, 1984, p. 11.

33 Mulvey, 'Notes on Sirk and melodrama', p. 54.

34 When a soap opera is terminated it is not because the narrative has run out, but mostly for external, commercial or organizational reasons. The narrative must then be turned off in an arbitrary way, which is usually very unsatisfactory for viewers: questions always remain open, narrative lines broken off.

35 Modleski, 'The search for tomorrow . . .', p. 12.

36 Barthes, *S/Z*, p. 76.

37 E. Seiter, 'Promise and contradiction: the daytime television serials', in *Filmreader 5*, Evanston, 1982, p. 158.

38 Modleski, 'The search for tomorrow . . .', p. 14.

39 M. J. Arlen, 'Smooth pebbles at Southfork', in M. J. Arlen (ed.), *The Camera Age*, Farrar, Straus & Giroux, New York, 1981.

40 Johnston, 'Crossroads . . .', p. 11.

41 Modleski, 'The search for tomorrow . . .', p. 14.

42 H. Newcomb, 'Texas: a giant state of mind', *Channels of Communication*, April/May, 1981, p. 41.

43 Newcomb, *TV: The Most Popular Art*, p. 178.

44 Brunsdon, 'Crossroads . . .', p. 36. The concepts cultural competence and cultural capital are borrowed from Pierre Bourdieu.

45 P. Brooks, 'The melodramatic imagination. The example of Balzac and James', in D. Thornburn and G. Hartman (eds), *Romanticism. Vistas, Instances, Continuities*, Cornell University Press, Ithaca/London, 1973, p. 218.
See also P. Brooks, *The Melodramatic Imagination*, Yale University Press, New Haven, 1976.

46 Brooks, 'The melodramatic imagination', p. 219.

47 ibid., p. 211.

48 V. Morin, 'The television serial: life in slow motion', in *Il Feuilleton in Televisione*, RAI, Venice, 1977, p. 48.

49 Cf. Brunsdon, 'Crossroads . . .'; according to Brunsdon soap opera demands cultural competences which in our culture are mainly possessed by women.

50 But each person acquires so many divergent experiences and impressions that it is impossible to process them all in a theoretically consistent and logical system. On the contrary, the daily

consciousness does not concern itself with (rational) logic. Antonio Gramsci pointed this out in his notes on 'common sense': A. Gramsci, *Selections from the Prison Notebooks*, Lawrence & Wishart, London, 1973.

51 Barthes, *The Pleasure of the Text*, p. 52.
52 ibid., p. 61.

Chapter 3

1 For a more general view of the negative reception by European intellectuals of the rise of American popular culture after the Second World War, see D. Hebdige, 'Towards a cartography of taste, 1935–1962', *Block*, no. 4, 1981, pp. 39–56.
2 J. Bardoel, J. Bierhoff, B. Manschot, P. Vasterman, *Marges in de media*, Het Wereldvenster, Baarn, 1975, pp. 58–9.
3 T. Eagleton, 'Ideology, fiction, narrative', *Social Text*, no. 2, 1979, p. 64.
4 For an evaluation of mass culture theories, see A. Swingewood, *The Myth of Mass Culture*, Macmillan, Basingstoke, 1977.
5 In *De Volkskrant*, 14 November 1981 (my italics).
6 M. Foucault, *L'Ordre du discours*, Gallimard, Paris, 1971.
7 S. Freud, *Jokes and the Relationship to the Unconscious*, Penguin, Harmondsworth, 1976, p. 232.
8 G. Therborn, *The Ideology of Power and the Power of Ideology*, Verso, London, 1980, p. 27.
9 ibid., p. 28.
10 For a more general survey of populism see E. Laclau, *Politics and Ideology in Marxist Theory*, Verso, London, 1977, chapter 4.
11 The difference between practical ideology and theoretical ideology is made *inter al.* by L. Althusser in *Philosophie et philosophie spontanée des savants*, Maspero, Paris, 1974. The Gramscian distinction between 'philosophy' and 'common sense' also links up with this.
12 Compare Bourdieu, 'The aristocracy of culture', pp. 243–4.
13 Frankie Goes To Hollywood, *Welcome to the Pleasure Dome*, Island, 1984.
14 Bourdieu, 'The aristocracy of culture', p. 237.

Chapter 4

1 See Seiter, 'Men, sex and money in recent family melodrama'.
2 See Modleski, 'The search for tomorrow . . .'.

3 These figures come from an enquiry by the Department for Viewing and Listening Research of the Dutch Broadcasting Foundation (May 1982).

4 ibid.

5 T. Modleski, *Loving with a Vengeance. Mass-Produced Fantasies for Women*, Shoe String Press, Hamden, 1982,/Methuen, London, 1984, p. 14.

6 Feuer, 'Melodrama, serial form and television today'.

7 ibid., p. 15.

8 E. Seiter, 'Eco's TV guide – the soaps', *Tabloid*, no. 5, winter 1982, p. 4.

9 For an analysis of the narrative strategies of the popular romantic novel, see Modleski, *Loving with a Vengeance*, chapter 2.

10 M. Barrett, 'Feminism and the definition of cultural politics', in R. Brunt and C. Rowan (eds), *Feminism, Culture and Politics*, Lawrence & Wishart, London, 1982, p. 56.

11 ibid., p. 57.

12 T. Lovell, 'Ideology and Coronation Street', in Dyer *et al.*, *Coronation Street*, p. 51.

Index